The Unofficial
Wizard's
Cookbook with Pictures

100+ Amazing Wizard's Recipes Inspired by the Films

Margie Valadez

Table of Contents

Introduction

Welcome! Young wizards, witches, and non-magical folk alike! In this cookbook, you will find magical and fantastic recipes inspired by what students might eat in the big hall at Hogwarts, plus some other meal ideas that wizards and witches in training might eat at other magic schools around the world. A young boy wizard is an orphan who forced to stay with his uncle and aunt. Soon he realizes he has some extraordinary powers, and he is taken to the wizard school of Hogwarts by Hagrid. He learns that his parents were killed by a dark wizard named Voldemort. Wizard (a young orphan boy) tries to kill Voldemort to revenge for his parent's death and save the Wizard world. All of the stories revolve around a young boy wizard who, at age 11, discovers that he has magical power. Harry was invited to sharpen his wizard skill at the "Hogwarts School of Witchcraft and Wizardry," where his befriends Ron Weasly and Hermione Granger. In this cookbook, you will find delicious wizard-inspired recipes that have easy cooking instructions. You can choose your favorite wizard recipe and prepare it for parties. Wizard recipes are perfect for any party to make magical. Whip up a mug of butter beer for your movie night. No matter the occasion, these delicious meals will make it much better!

Welcome to the Magical Food World!

History of Magic

This series is about a young orphan boy whose parents are murdered. He didn't know he was a wizard. At Hogwarts, he learns magic and forms a strong bond with his friends. Lord Voldemort killed his parents. His goal is to defeat Voldemort. Voldemort tries to kill him, but he survives and fights with Voldemort with his sharp mind. This series has been translated into seventy languages. This series was published in 1997.

Wizard-inspired Recipes

In this series, I love broom, sorting hat, elder wands, deathly hallow, spiders, owls, howler, wizard birthday cake, toads, golden snitch ball, wizard chess, and many more. So, I thought to the baked wizard-inspired recipes. Then, I prepared golden snitch peanut balls, chocolate frog, spider cookies, wizard cake, sorting hat, broomstick, and other yummy wizard-inspired recipes.

Top Magical Food at the Wizard World

In the wizard series, these are the top magical and delicious food eaten on different occasions.

Frozen Butterbeer: What is butterbeer made of? The ingredient list to make this delicious drink is short and easy! There are a few ingredients you will need to prepare. These are the followings: vanilla ice cream, cream soda, butterscotch ice cream, and whipped cream for topping. Easy!

Shepherd's Pie: Shepherd's pie is a traditional English meat pie that consists of lamb and vegetables and is then covered in mashed potatoes. It was served at dinner at Hogwarts School of Witchcraft and Wizardry.

Pumpkin Fizz: Pumpkin Fizz is a yummy and popular drink in the wizard series. The taste of this drink is the same as pumpkin pie soda. You will get hints of cinnamon, nutmeg, and apple cider.

Sticky Toffee Pudding: It is a magical sticky toffee pudding for wizard series fans. It is a traditional British dessert that consists of chopped dates, toffee sauce, sponge cake, and top with vanilla ice cream. Toffee Pudding is one of the all-time favorite desserts in the wizarding world.

Chocolate Frog: Enjoy wizard chocolate frog at home! It is a very popular wizard sweet made up of chocolate in a frog shape. It is covered in a pentagonal box.

Beef Sunday Roast: It is served on Sunday night at Hogwarts hall. Perfectly roasted in the oven!

Wizard Poem

I love the wizard series
Like wizard loves his parents
Like Dumbledore loves Hogwarts
Like Dobby loves socks
It is a time to love baking food
Like Luna love to eat puddings
Like Ron wants a lot of food
It is time of thinking
Flying, catching, magic
All things are puzzling
Like Hogwarts school
All stories revolve around the wizard!

What to Serve at Your Hogwarts Dinner Feast

The cookbook contains plenty of incredible food the characters enjoyed; you can prepare them all at home! Whether you are celebrating a Wizard Birthday party, the Return to Hogwarts School, or just having a fun party, here are some ideas of what you can serve at your wizard-inspired party! You can select from this cookbook if you are looking for simple dinner recipes for a wizard theme party. There are a few other Hogwarts feasts throughout the series: Christmas feast, Halloween feast, and last day of the feast. Each of the Hogwarts feasts is loaded with mouthwatering foods. The Hogwarts feast includes foods like roast beef and roast chicken, boiled and roasted potatoes, Yorkshire pudding, peas, carrots, and gravy. The Sunday roast is a British cuisine and of course Hogwarts dinner table. Two important things to remember while cooking it: marinate your meat well and don't overcook it. There are all types of potato recipes in the wizard series: for example, mashed, baked, and roasted. Mashed potato is one of the most popular dish in the wizard world.

Wizard Essentials

The Great Hall:

The great hall is a prominent and impressive part of Hogwarts. The main gathering area in Hogwarts is where breakfast, lunch, and dinner are held. Breakfast is from 7:30 AM to 8:50 AM, lunch is from 11:45 AM to 12:45 PM, and dinner is from 7:35 PM till 8:35 PM. Other special events, like Halloween parties, are also held and receive daily owl posts.

Floating Candles:

The floating candles are one of the most memorable parts of the series. Whether you are having a wizard party or want to do something fun for Halloween or a movie night, you can't go wrong with these simple DIY Wizard Floating Candles.

Floating Pumpkins:

The great hall is full of floating pumpkins at the Halloween party. They look amazing. On that day, a great dinner will hold with delicious foods.

Four Types of Tables:

Gryffindor table: It has red and golden colors. The chair, napkins, and red table runner should be red color. Cutlery and gold chargers finished the table setting.

Slytherin table: It has silver and green colors. The runner, napkins, goblets, and chair sashes are green. Cutlery and silver chargers finished the table setting.

Hufflepuff table: It has black and yellow colors. Plates were black on the table. The runner, napkins, and chair sashes are yellow.

Ravenclaw table: It has bronze and blue colors. A blue runner, napkins and chair sashes were paired with blue water glasses as well as gold chargers and cutlery to complete this table setting.

Questions for Your Kids if They Love Wizard Series

You can ask these interesting questions around the dinner table, on a road trip, or after watching the wizard series.

Would you steal the dragon's egg or save your friend from the mermaids?

Would you purchase a pygmy puff or a love potion?

Would you want to travel on the knight bus or by floo powder?

Would you drink pumpkin juice or butterbeer?

Would you travel by thestral or portkey?

Would you want to drink Veritaserum or Polyjuice

Potion?

Would you want to meet dementors in the alley or Aragog in the forest?

Would you want to go to the Yule ball or Christmas party?

Would you want to fight with Nagini or Basilisk?

Would you want to play wizard chess for Exploding Snap?

Would you want to collect Chocolate Frog cards or Gobstones?

Would you want to transform into a dog, a rat, or a cat?

Would you want to eat Pumpkin Pasties or Cauldron Cakes?

Would you want to dance with Madam Maxine or Hagrid?

Would you rather speak Mermish or Parseltongue?

Would you want to destroy the diary or Slytherin's locket?

Would you want to spend the night in the Shrieking Shack or the Forbidden Forest?

Would you want to wear Ron's dress robes or a Weasley sweater?

FAQ

What are famous foods from the wizard series?

Answer: These are following food from the wizard series.

- Butterbeer
- Shepherd's pie
- Pumpkin pasties
- Treacle tarts
- Wizard birthday cake from Hagrid
- Molly's meat pies
- Kreacher's French Onion Soup
- Pumpkin juice
- Rock cakes

What do you serve at the wizard dinner?

Answer: Hogwarts feast is filled with potatoes, vegetables, and meats, such as shepherd's pie. For dessert, the wizard's favorite dish is treacle tart.

What kind of food is at the wizard party?

Answer: A wizard party may serve food such as butterbeer-flavor-like cookies, cupcakes, cake, drinks, pudding, rock cakes, pudding, pastries, treacle tarts, shepherd's pie, and many more.

Wizard Magical Gifts:

These are famous wizard gifts you can create for your kids.

Wizard Mug

Quidditch

Wand Night Light

Wizard Makeup Brushes

Wizard Shirt

Playing Cards

Dobby Socks

Wizard Glasses

Sorting Hat

Magical Recipe Terms

Bake: To cook food in an oven over medium heat.

Al dente: Cook food until firm – not crunchy and not too soft.

Beat: To stir well until a mixture is smooth. You can do this with a spoon, whisk, or a mixer.

Baste: To add moisture to food while cooking it.

Braise: To brown first, then simmer food over low heat in a small amount of liquid. The pan should be covered. This results in tender meat.

Boil: To cook in water that has reached 212 degrees Fahrenheit.

Blanch: To boil fruit or veggie for a short time to seal in color and flavor.

Brown: To cook on high heat to add a darker color to the food.

Broil: To cook on a rack under direct heat. You can do this in an oven.

Caramelized: To beat sugar until it melts and turns into syrup. The syrup can look golden, brown, or even dark brown.

Cream: To beat ingredients together until smooth.

Chop: To cut food into small pieces.

Cube: To cut food into pieces that is around ½-inch wide.

Dice: To cut food into very small pieces, around ⅛-inch wide. Dice means smaller pieces than chop.

Fold: To gently use a spatula to mix dry ingredients into wet ingredients.

Dust: To lightly cover a dessert with powdered sugar or dust a surface or dough with flour before rolling.

Dredge: To coat uncooked food with bread crumbs, flour, or other mixture.

Dash: ⅛ teaspoon

Glaze: To coat food in sauce, icing, or other spread.

Zest: To grate the outer peel of citrus fruits.

Whisk: To incorporate air into a mixture or to combine dry ingredients until smooth, using a fork or a whisk.

Whip: To incorporate air into the mixture using a whisk or mixer.

To taste: Season a dish with salt and pepper, as you like.

Stew: On low heat, cook ingredients in liquid, usually in a covered pan.

Slice: To cut ingredients into similar-sized thin pieces.

Simmer: To cook a liquid just below the boiling point. You'll see bubbles forming, but they aren't bursting on the surface.

Shred: To cut food into narrow strips. You can use a knife or a grater to do this.

Sauté: Also called pan-fry, sauté means to cook food using a small amount of oil over high heat.

Roast: To cook meat or veggies in dry heat in an oven.

Poach: To cook over low heat, with liquid just barely simmering.

Pinch: 1/16 teaspoon

Mince: To cut ingredients into small pieces.

Knead: Mix the dough using your hands or a mixer.

Grate: To process the food using a grater.

Snack Recipes

Mini Dark Wizards

Prep Time: 20 minutes|Cook Time: 30 minutes|Servings: 15

Ingredients:

2 cups white chocolate
½ can condensed milk
1 teaspoon vanilla extract
1 pack brownie mix
2 eggs
⅓ cup oil
¼ cup water
Red food coloring
Black food coloring
Toothpicks

Preparation:

1. Make the brownie mix according to the packet directions.
2. Heat the chocolate and condensed milk in a saucepan over low heat until mixed.
3. Remove from the heat and stir in the vanilla extract. Freeze the mixture for 10 minutes.
4. When the brownies are finished, shape them into round cone-like bodies about 2 inches tall for the base.
5. Insert a toothpick through the center of each "body" to serve as a connecting piece for the head.
6. Once the condensed milk and chocolate mixture has cooled, scoop and smooth it into 1-inch balls to make the "heads."
7. Push a head down onto the toothpick poking out of the body to secure it.
8. Make red eyes using the red food coloring and a toothpick. Create the nostrils using the black food coloring and another toothpick.
9. Serve and enjoy!

Serving Suggestions: Serve with black sprinkles on top.
Variation Tip: You can also use store-bought brownies.
Nutritional Information per Serving:
Calories: 383|Fat: 19g|Sat Fat: 6g|Carbohydrates: 50g|Fiber: 0.1g|Sugar: 19g|Protein: 4g

Golden Flying Balls

Prep Time: 20 minutes|Cook Time: 5 minutes|Servings: 25

Ingredients:

1 cup marshmallows
8 cups Rice Krispies
1 tablespoon butter
1 cup white chocolate, melted
Yellow sugar sprinkles

Preparation:

1. Spread the butter all over the inside of a big mixing bowl, then add the marshmallows. Microwave for 45 seconds or until the marshmallows have completely melted.
2. Add the Rice Krispies to the bowl a cup at a time, mixing well after each addition.
3. Roll the mixture into 2-inch balls and roll them in the sugar sprinkles. Place them on a baking sheet and set them aside.
4. Put the melted white chocolate into a piping bag.
5. Pipe out enough pairs of wings to equal the number of balls onto a sheet of parchment paper and place them in the refrigerator to cool. Remove them from the refrigerator when they're firm.
6. Place a wing on either side of a ball.
7. Serve and enjoy!

Serving Suggestions: Serve with sprinkles on top.
Variation Tip: You can use any puffed rice cereal you prefer.
Nutritional Information per Serving:
Calories: 50|Fat: 0.6g|Sat Fat: 0g|Carbohydrates: 10g|Fiber: 0g|Sugar: 1g|Protein: 0.8g

Giant's Bath Buns

Prep Time: 15 minutes|Cook Time: 20 minutes|Servings: 12

Ingredients:

2 sticks unsalted butter

1 tablespoon caraway seeds

12 sugar cubes

1 large whole egg, beaten

8 ounces milk, warmed

2¼ teaspoons dry yeast

3½ cups all-purpose flour

1 teaspoon salt

2 tablespoons granulated sugar

Preparation:

1. Mix the warm milk and yeast in a bowl and set aside for 10 minutes.
2. In a mixer, combine the flour, salt, and sugar and blend until combined. Mix in the butter on medium speed until the mixture resembles breadcrumbs.
3. Use a dough hook to incorporate the yeast mixture and caraway seeds. Mix until everything is combined. Allow it to sit for 10 minutes.
4. Set the mixer to medium speed. Knead until the dough forms a smooth ball, and the basin's edges are clean.
5. Cover and set aside in a warm place for 45 minutes or until the dough has doubled in size.
6. Preheat the oven to 375°F. Divide the dough into 12 equal-sized pieces and place it on a lightly floured surface.
7. Make each piece of dough into a sphere and press a sugar cube into the seam side. Pinch the seam closed and roll back into a ball form.
8. Place them seam side down on a baking sheet and cover with a moist cloth. Put the baking sheet in a warm place for 30 minutes until the dough has proofed and doubled in size.
9. Once proofed, brush the buns with the egg and bake for 15–20 minutes, or until golden brown.
10. Serve and enjoy!

Serving Suggestions: Serve with jam.
Variation Tip: You can also serve with buttercream.
Nutritional Information per Serving:
Calories: 307|Fat: 16g|Sat Fat: 10g|Carbohydrates: 37g|Fiber: 1g|Sugar: 7g|Protein: 5g

Licorice Wands

Prep Time: 10 minutes|Cook Time: 0 minutes|Servings: 12

Ingredients:

6 ounces vanilla-flavored candy coating

24 licorice twists

Preparation:

1. Put the candy coating in a small bowl and microwave until melted.
2. Coat one-third to one-half of the licorice twists with the candy coating.
3. Serve and enjoy!

Serving Suggestions: Garnish with sprinkles on top.
Variation Tip: You can use melted white chocolate for the coating.
Nutritional Information per Serving:
Calories: 78|Fat: 3g|Sat Fat: 2g|Carbohydrates: 10g|Fiber: 0g|Sugar: 9g|Protein: 0g

Vanilla Butter Beer Cookies

Prep Time: 20 minutes|Cook Time: 25 minutes|Servings: 14

Ingredients
Cookies

1¼ cups all-purpose flour
¼ teaspoon salt
½ cup unsalted butter, room temperature

½ cup powdered sugar
¼ teaspoon vanilla extract
½ teaspoon butter extract

Ganache

½ cup heavy cream
5½ ounces butterscotch chips

Instructions
1. Preheat the oven to 350°F and line your baking trays with parchment paper. Set aside.
2. In a medium bowl, combine together the flour and salt and set aside.
3. With your mixer, cream together the butter, powdered sugar, butter extract and vanilla extract until light and fluffy. Add all the dry ingredients and mix on low speed for about a minute.
4. Wipe down the sides of the bowl and increase the speed to medium, and mix for another minute until a dough forms.
5. Scoop a tablespoon of dough at a time and roll it into a ball and place the balls on your baking tray about 1½ inches apart. You can use the back of a teaspoon to make an indention in the cookie. Bake for 10 minutes.
6. After 10 minutes, remove the cookies from the oven and immediately press down the indention a bit more to hold the ganache.
7. Return the cookies to the oven and continue to bake for another 10 minutes. Transfer cookies to a wire rack to cool completely.

Ganache: Place your butterscotch chips in a bowl and set aside. In a small saucepan on medium heat, heat the heavy cream up to just before a boil.
Remove from heat and pour over the butterscotch chips. Allow to sit for a minute or so and whisk until smooth. You need to allow the ganache to cool to room temperature before using it.

Assembly: When the cookies have cooled, pipe the ganache into the center of each cookie.
Drizzle the top with additional ganache if you want. Allow the ganache to set and enjoy.

Serving Suggestion: Serve topped with additional ganache drizzling.
Variation Tip: Sprinkle icing sugar for a velvety touch.
Nutritional Information Per Serving:
Calories 84|Carbohydrates 13g|Protein 1g|Fat 3g|Sodium 75mg|Fiber 2g

Magic Broomsticks

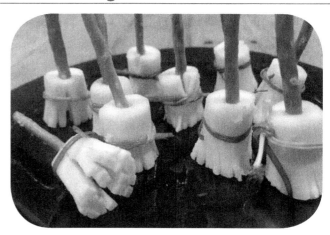

Prep Time: 10 minutes|Cook Time: 5 minutes|Servings: 8

Ingredients:
2 sticks string cheese   ½ cup chives
8 pretzel sticks

Preparation:
1. Cut each string cheese horizontally into four equal pieces. These will be the bottom of the "broomsticks."
2. Make small cuts along one end of each piece, then turn 90° and repeat to produce a ragged look at the bottom.
3. Press a pretzel stick into the non-frayed end of the cheese to keep it together.
4. Tie a chive around the broomstick's "base" and the cheese closest to the side with the pretzel to finish the look.
5. Serve and enjoy!

Serving Suggestions: Serve with fries.
Variation Tip: You can use any hard cheese you prefer.
Nutritional Information per Serving:
Calories: 20|Fat: 0.1g|Sat Fat: 0g|Carbohydrates: 0.1g|Fiber: 0.1g|Sugar: 0.1g|Protein: 0.2g

Butter Beer Sugar Cookies

Prep Time: 20 minutes|Cook Time: 30 minutes|Servings: 24

Ingredients

¾ cup butter, cubed, at room temperature
¾ cup packed brown sugar
½ cup white sugar
1 large egg
2 tablespoons maple syrup
2 tablespoons sour cream
2 teaspoons vanilla butter

nut flavoring
½ teaspoon pumpkin pie spice
2 teaspoons baking soda
2 cups all-purpose flour
2 tablespoons white sugar, or as needed

Preparations

1. Beat butter, brown sugar, and white sugar together in a large bowl until creamy. Add egg, maple syrup, sour cream, vanilla butter and nut flavoring, and pumpkin pie spice. Mix again until combined.
2. Add baking soda and slowly mix in flour, ½ cup at a time; the dough will be sticky.
3. Chill dough in the refrigerator for 30 minutes.
4. Preheat the oven to 350°F.
5. Pour 2 tablespoons of white sugar into a shallow bowl. Roll dough into walnut-sized balls using your hands, roll balls in sugar, and place on an ungreased cookie sheet.
6. Flatten each cookie slightly using your palm, and leave space between each, as cookies will spread during baking.
7. Bake in the preheated oven until edges are golden brown, 8 to 10 minutes. Cool on a rack.

Serving Suggestion: Serve cookies topped with butter beer ganache.
Variation Tip: Use chocolate topping inside the cookies.

Nutritional Information Per Serving:
Calories 145|Carbohydrates 21.2g|Protein 1.4g|Fat 6.3g|Sodium 151.6mg|Fiber 0.3g

Wizard's Beer Jello Shots

Prep Time: 10 minutes|Cook Time: 5 minutes|Servings: 18

Ingredients:

1 cup butterscotch schnapps
2 cups cream soda
3 tablespoons unflavored

gelatin
1 cup caramel vodka
Whipped cream, for garnish

Preparation:

1. Put the cream soda in a medium saucepan. Add the gelatin and whisk until it's dissolved. Let the mixture sit for 2–3 minutes.
2. Heat the mixture over medium-low heat until it becomes steamy.
3. Stir in the butterscotch schnapps.
4. Then, add the caramel vodka and whisk once more.
5. Evenly pour the mixture into 2-ounce jello shot cups.
6. Let the shots chill for at least 4 hours in the refrigerator.
7. Drizzle with butterscotch syrup after topping with whipped cream.
8. Serve and enjoy!

Serving Suggestions: Add some sprinkles on top.
Variation Tip: You can also use maple syrup.
Nutritional Information per Serving:
Calories: 80|Fat: 0g|Sat Fat: 0g|Carbohydrates: 9g|Fiber: 0g|Sugar: 9g|Protein: 1g

Pumpkin Pasties

Prep Time: 20 minutes|Cook Time: 15 minutes|Servings: 10

Ingredients:

Refrigerated pie dough
¼ can pumpkin puree
2 cloves garlic, finely chopped
⅛ teaspoon dried sage
⅛ teaspoon salt
⅛ teaspoon pepper
1 tablespoon butter, melted
1 teaspoon butter, at room temperature
A few chopped chives
⅓ cup cheese, shredded

Preparation:

1. Combine the pumpkin puree, room temperature butter, salt, pepper, garlic, sage, and cheese in a large mixing bowl.
2. Preheat the oven to 400°F.
3. Spread out the dough and cut out 5–to 6-inch circles, working quickly and keeping the dough moist.
4. Peel apart each layer from each circle and brush between each one with the melted butter to prevent burning and ensure even baking. Place on a baking sheet lined with parchment paper.
5. Place a large teaspoon of the pumpkin filling in the center, then fold the dough to form a semi-circle, similar to a dumpling.
6. Bake the pasties in the preheated oven for 12 minutes.
7. Serve and enjoy!

Serving Suggestions: Serve with ketchup on the side.
Variation Tip: You can also add chopped vegetables inside the pasties.
Nutritional Information per Serving:
Calories: 27|Fat: 2g|Sat Fat: 1g|Carbohydrates: 0.3g|Fiber: 0g|Sugar: 0.1g|Protein: 1g

Butterbeer Caramelized Popcorn

Prep Time: 5 minutes|Cook Time: 10 minutes|Servings: 5

Ingredients:

3½ tablespoons butter
2 heaped tablespoons corn syrup
1 teaspoon pumpkin pie spice
½ cup British ale
¼ cup popcorn kernels
¾ cup packed brown sugar

Preparation:

1. Fill a brown paper lunch bag halfway with popcorn kernels, fold the top over, and seal with microwave-safe tape. Microwave on high for about 2 minutes.
2. Put the popcorn into a large glass bowl.
3. Preheat the oven to 260°F.
4. Line a baking sheet with parchment paper.
5. Combine the ale, sugar, corn syrup, and butter in a medium saucepan. Bring the mixture to a boil, then let it simmer until it becomes hard and starts to crack.
6. Remove the pan from the heat, stir in the pumpkin pie spice, and pour it over the popcorn.
7. Stir thoroughly, then pour the mixture onto the baking sheet and place it in the oven.
8. Bake for 40 minutes, then set it aside to cool.
9. Serve and enjoy!

Serving Suggestions: Sprinkle more pumpkin spice on top.
Variation Tip: You can use any ale you prefer.
Nutritional Information per Serving:
Calories: 209|Fat: 8g|Sat Fat: 9g|Carbohydrates: 35g|Fiber: 1g|Sugar: 23g|Protein: 1g

Skewered Basilisks

Prep Time: 10 minutes|Cook Time: 20 minutes|Servings: 12

Ingredients:

11 ounces refrigerated breadstick dough
¼ teaspoon butter, melted

Herbs or spices, to taste
½ pimiento, sliced
Black olives, sliced

Preparation:
1. Preheat the oven to 350°F.
2. Spray 12 wooden BBQ skewers with nonstick spray.
3. Wrap breadstick dough around each skewer and flatten the ends slightly.
4. To make the "eyes," lay two black olive slices on the top of the flat end and a small piece of pimiento under the eyes for the "tongue."
5. Place the skewers on a baking sheet lined with parchment paper and bake in the preheated oven for 20 minutes or until the breadsticks are golden brown.
6. Remove from the oven and immediately brush with the melted butter, then brush with any herbs or spices of your choice. Allow cooling before serving.
7. Enjoy!

Serving Suggestions: Sprinkle with sea salt flakes instead of herbs or spices.
Variation Tip: Make your own dough from scratch and add green food coloring.
Nutritional Information per Serving:
Calories: 44|Fat: 1g|Sat Fat: 0.1g|Carbohydrates: 22g|Fiber: 2.2g|Sugar: 7g|Protein: 3g

Acid Pops

Prep Time: 10 minutes|Cook Time: 0 minutes|Servings: 12

Ingredients:

12 lollipops
½ cup pop rocks

¼ cup honey

Preparation:
1. Place the pop rocks into a small bowl.
2. Heat the honey in a small bowl for 20–30 seconds in the microwave.
3. Coat the lollipops with the heated honey, then coat them with the pop rocks. If the honey thickens, reheat it. Place the lollipops on wax paper to dry.
4. Serve and enjoy!

Serving Suggestions: Garnish with sprinkles on top.
Variation Tip: You can use any flavor lollipop you prefer.
Nutritional Information per Serving:
Calories: 22|Fat: 0g|Sat Fat: 0g|Carbohydrates: 6g|Fiber: 0g|Sugar: 5g|Protein: 0g

Desserts and Sweet Treats

Harry Birthday Cake

Prep Time: 15 minutes|Cook Time: 30 minutes|Servings: 15

Ingredients:
1 vanilla cake mix
14 ounces cream cheese frosting
3 drops red food coloring
Green icing pen

Preparation:
1. Bake the cake according to the packet directions. Set it aside to cool.
2. Mix the cream cheese frosting with the red food coloring to make a medium pink.
3. Once the cake has cooled, apply a uniform layer of pink frosting to the top, forming waves with your knife.
4. Crookedly write "HAPPEE BIRTHDAE HARRY" on the top with the green icing pen.
5. To create a cracked effect on the cake, drag a knife or toothpick down from between the P and E of "HAPPEE," to between the H and D of "BIRTHDAE," and lastly between the H and A of "HARRY."
6. Serve and enjoy!

Serving Suggestions: Serve with black sprinkles on top.
Variation Tip: You can use any flavor of cake mix you prefer.
Nutritional Information per Serving:
Calories: 260|Fat: 2g|Sat Fat: 3g|Carbohydrates: 3g|Fiber: 2g|Sugar: 19g|Protein: 0.2g

Butterbeer Cupcakes

Prep Time: 10 minutes|Cook Time: 15 minutes|Servings: 12

Ingredients:
For the cake:
1 box vanilla cake mix

For the frosting:
1 cup butter, at room temp
3 cups icing sugar mixture
1 tablespoon milk
¼ cup caramel topping

Preparation:
1. Preheat the oven to the specified temperature as per the packet instructions for baking cupcakes.
2. Use paper liners to line a cupcake tray.
3. Prepare the cake mix according to the packet directions and bake for the specified time in the preheated oven.
4. Allow 5 minutes in the tray before transferring to a wire rack to cool.
5. Beat the butter in a bowl for 2 minutes.
6. Add in the icing sugar and whisk.
7. Gradually whisk in the milk and 2 tablespoons of the caramel topping until the frosting is smooth and thoroughly blended. If the frosting is too stiff, add one additional tablespoon of milk.
8. Once the cakes have completely cooled, pipe the frosting on top using a large open star tip (1M) or as desired.
9. Serve and enjoy!

Serving Suggestions: Drizzle with the remaining caramel topping.
Variation Tip: Add some mini white chocolate chips for crunch.
Nutritional Information per Serving:
Calories: 686|Fat: 23g|Sat Fat: 13g|Carbohydrates: 11g|Fiber: 1g|Sugar: 82g|Protein: 4g

Butterscotch Cupcakes

Prep Time: 30 minutes|Cook Time: 20 minutes+30 minutes cooling time|Servings: 18

Ingredients

Cupcake

2 cups flour	12 ounces/1 can cream soda
1 cup sugar	3.4 ounces/1 pack
2 teaspoons baking powder	butterscotch pudding
½ teaspoon salt	

Frosting

2 cups powdered sugar	whipping cream
½ cup unsalted butter	3 tablespoons butterscotch
2 tablespoons heavy	sauce

Preparation

1. Preheat oven to 350°F. Line cupcake pan with liners.
2. Mix together the flour, sugar, baking powder, and salt.
3. Add cream soda and beat until thoroughly blended.
4. Add the butterscotch pudding, mix and stir well.
5. Pour the batter into the lined cupcake pan until ¾-full.
6. Bake at 350°F for 15 to 20 minutes. Allow cupcakes to cool for at least 30 minutes before frosting.
7. Frosting.
8. Mix butter with powdered sugar until small pebbles appear.
9. Add whipping cream and beat slowly. (It should hold a stiff peak.)
10. Frost the cupcakes as wanted.

Serving Suggestion: Serve cold topped with butterscotch sauce.

Variation Tip: Use butterscotch candy chunks for a crunch.
Nutritional Information Per Serving
Calories 247|Carbohydrates 45g|Protein 2g|Fat 7g|Sodium 107mg|Fiber 1g

Tempting Treacle Tart

Prep Time: 20 minutes|Cook Time: 45 minutes|Servings: 4

Ingredients:

2 sheets frozen ready-made	1 cup golden syrup
shortcrust pastry	5 ounces fresh white
2 lemons, juiced	breadcrumbs

Preparation:

1. Defrost the shortcrust pastry at room temperature.
2. Preheat the oven to 320°F.
3. Line a greased 9-inch loose-bottomed tart pan with a defrosted pastry sheet. (Use two if one isn't enough.)
4. Prick the base of the pastry with a fork. Set it aside (or chill it in the refrigerator).
5. Warm the golden syrup in a saucepan over low heat, stirring in the lemon zest, juice, and breadcrumbs.
6. Fill the pastry case with the filling and bake for 45 minutes–1 hour, or until set.
7. Serve and enjoy!

Serving Suggestions: Serve with whipping cream or ice cream.
Variation Tip: You can create a lattice pattern on top of the tart before baking using more pastry. To help the tart to brown, brush the lattice with an egg wash.
Nutritional Information per Serving:
Calories: 119|Fat: 3g|Sat Fat: 2g|Carbohydrates: 20g|Fiber: 1g|Sugar: 10g|Protein: 3g

Mystical Mini Tarts

Prep Time: 30 minutes|Cook Time: 12 minutes|Servings: 24

Ingredients:
For the pastry:

½ cup almond meal	1 egg
¾ teaspoon salt	½ cup sugar
½ teaspoon baking powder	10 tablespoons unsalted
1½ cups flour	butter

For the filling:

1 cup golden syrup	2 tablespoons lemon juice
1 teaspoon vanilla extract	⅛ cup breadcrumbs
1 tablespoon butter	Freshly whipped cream, for
1 egg	topping
1 tablespoon heavy cream	

Preparation:
1. Mix the butter and sugar in a large bowl. Beat in the egg until fully combined.
2. Sift the flour into a separate bowl. Mix in the almond meal, salt, and baking powder.
3. Add the dry ingredients to the wet components and mix on low until a dough forms.
4. Wrap the dough in plastic wrap and place it in the refrigerator for 1–2 hours.
5. Preheat the oven to 400°F.
6. Fill miniature tart pans halfway with the dough. Ensure that the bottoms and sides are evenly covered.
7. Warm the golden syrup in a small saucepan over low heat. Remove from the heat and whisk in the butter until melted. Allow for a few minutes of cooling.
8. Mix the egg and cream in a small bowl, then stir into the syrup mixture.
9. Stir in the vanilla extract, breadcrumbs, and lemon juice until well-mixed.
10. Fill the pastry shells halfway with the mixture. If you fill them more than halfway, they will overflow when baking.
11. Bake for 10–12 minutes or until the crusts are golden brown.
12. Allow cooling on a wire rack before serving.
13. Enjoy!

Serving Suggestions: Top with fresh whipped cream.
Variation Tip: You can also add chopped nuts.
Nutritional Information per Serving:
Calories: 177|Fat: 7g|Sat Fat: 4g|Carbohydrates: 26g|Fiber: 0.6g|Sugar: 9.6g|Protein: 9g

Candy Witch Brooms

Prep Time: 10 minutes|Cook Time: 0 minutes|Servings: 10

Ingredients:

10 mini chocolate peanut butter cups	10 pretzel sticks

Preparation:
1. Use a toothpick to pierce the bottom of each peanut butter cup to make a hole for the pretzel sticks.
2. Insert one pretzel stick into each hole, but not too far since you don't want it to come out the other side of the cup.
3. Serve and enjoy!

Serving Suggestions: Garnish with butterscotch syrup.
Variation Tip: You can use any mini chocolate cups you prefer.
Nutritional Information per Serving:
Calories: 40|Fat: 3g|Sat Fat: 0g|Carbohydrates: 0.1g|Fiber: 0g|Sugar: 5g|Protein: 0g

Sleeping Draught Cakes

Prep Time: 15 minutes|Cook Time: 20 minutes|Servings: 6

Ingredients:

6 tablespoons butter, softened
½ cup granulated sugar
2 eggs

1 teaspoon baking powder
1 teaspoon salt
1 cup all-purpose flour, sifted

For the buttercream filling:
5½ tablespoons butter, softened
2¾ cups powdered sugar, sifted
1½ teaspoons chamomile

powder
1 tablespoon honey
2–3 tablespoons milk
Chocolate sprinkles, for topping

Preparation:

1. Preheat the oven to 350°F. Add the 6 tablespoons of softened butter to a mixer bowl and paddle until soft. Mix in the granulated sugar for 3 minutes.

2. Add the eggs one at a time, scraping in between. Add the sifted flour, baking powder, and salt in two additions. Mix to combine.

3. Pour the batter into a cupcake tray lined with liners.

4. Bake for 15–20 minutes until a skewer inserted into the center of each cupcake comes out clean. Allow the cakes to cool.

5. In a mixing bowl, soften the second amount of butter. Sift in the powdered sugar and chamomile powder. Mix until well blended.

6. Mix in the honey and milk.

7. Remove the cupcakes from their liners. Carefully cut a hole in the center of each cupcake with a paring knife.

8. Fill with just enough buttercream to hold the sprinkles in place.

9. Serve and enjoy!

Serving Suggestions: Top with chocolate sprinkles.
Variation Tip: You can also add chopped nuts as a topping.
Nutritional Information per Serving:
Calories: 568|Fat: 23g|Sat Fat: 15g|Carbohydrates: 85g|Fiber: 0.6g|Sugar: 60g|Protein: 7g

Yorkshire Pudding

Prep Time: 5 minutes|Cook Time: 30 minutes|Servings: 12

Ingredients

cooking spray or oil
½ cup flour
6 eggs

2 cups milk
1 teaspoon salt

Preparations

1. Preheat your oven to 445°F.

2. In a muffin tray, add in a bit of oil to each tin.

3. Place in the oven on the top shelf.

4. In a mixing bowl, whisk together the flour, eggs, milk, and salt until it's a thin mixture.

5. Once the oil in the tray is bubbling hot, add the mixture evenly into each muffin tin.

6. Place it back in the oven for 20 to 30 minutes until the Yorkshire puddings have risen and are golden brown.

Serving Suggestion: Serve warm along with roast pork chops.
Variation Tip: Use flavored oil for a more defined flavor.
Nutritional Information Per Serving:
Calories 124|Carbohydrates 18g|Protein 4g|Fat 4g|Sodium 90 mg|Fiber 1g

Halloween Triple Berry Pie

Prep Time: 20 minutes|Cook Time: 45 minutes|Servings: 12

Ingredients

2 homemade pie crusts for a 9-inch-deep dish pan.	1 tablespoon lemon juice
7 cups fresh raspberries, blueberries and blackberries	4 tablespoons cornstarch
	2 tablespoons butter
1 cup granulated sugar	1 large egg white

Preparation

Cook berries:

1. Add berries, sugar and lemon juice to a large saucepan over medium heat.
2. Simmer, until warm and juicy, about 5 to 10 minutes, gently stirring occasionally.

Thicken filling:

1. Spoon out about ½ cup of the juice from the pan into a bowl. Stir cornstarch into the juice until smooth.
2. Bring a pot of berries back to a simmer and slowly pour in the cornstarch. Gently stir the mixture, until thickened, about 2 to 5 minutes.
3. Remove from heat and stir in the butter. Allow to cool for 15 minutes. Pour mixture into unbaked pie shell.
4. Add lattice top or a whole top with holes pricked on top for steam to escape.
5. Pinch the edges of the top and bottom pie crusts together and crimp the edge, if you like. Brush a thin layer of beaten egg white over the top of the pie and sprinkle lightly with sugar.
6. Bake at 400°F for 40 to 45 minutes. Check it after 25 minutes and place a piece of tinfoil over it if the top crust is getting too brown.
7. Once done move to a wire cooling rack and allow cooling for several hours.

Serving Suggestion: Serve cool slices with ice cream.

Variation Tip: Use berries of your choice.
Nutritional Information Per Serving:
Calories 268|Carbohydrates 43g|Protein 2g|Fat 9g|Sodium 138mg|Fiber 3g

Mad-Eye Truffles

Prep Time: 10 minutes|Cook Time: 25 minutes|Servings: 12

Ingredients:

1 cup chocolate chips	1 teaspoon vanilla extract
½ can sweetened condensed milk	Blue icing pen
	Black icing pen
1 cup coconut powder	

Preparation:

1. Mix chocolate chips and condensed milk in a saucepan over low heat, then remove from the heat when smooth.
2. Add the vanilla essence, stir, and then place the mixture in the freezer for 6–8 minutes.
3. Roll the mixture into little balls (about 1-inch).
4. Roll them firmly in the coconut powder, ensuring the coconut sticks to all sides well.
5. Make the iris of the "eye" with the blue icing pen, and then draw a pupil in the middle with the black icing pen.
6. Put them in the freezer for 30 minutes before serving.
7. Enjoy!

Serving Suggestions: Serve with sprinkles on top.
Variation Tip: You can also add chopped nuts to the mixture.
Nutritional Information per Serving:
Calories: 77|Fat: 4g|Sat Fat: 3g|Carbohydrates: 8g|Fiber: 0g|Sugar: 7g|Protein: 1g

Enchanted New Year Eve Pumpkin Pie

Prep Time: 60 minutes|Cook Time: 60 minutes|Servings: 8

Ingredients:

2 large eggs plus the yolk of a third egg
½ cup packed dark brown sugar
⅓ cup white sugar
½ teaspoon salt
2 teaspoons cinnamon
1 teaspoon ground ginger
¼ teaspoon ground nutmeg
¼ teaspoon ground cloves
⅛ teaspoon ground cardamom

½ teaspoon lemon zest
2 cups pumpkin pulp purée from a sugar pumpkin (see Recipe Note) OR 1 15-ounce can of pumpkin purée (can also use puréed cooked butternut squash)
1 ½ cups heavy cream or one 12 oz. can of evaporated milk
1 good pie crust, chilled or frozen

Preparation:

1. Preheat your oven to 425°F
2. Beat the eggs in a large bowl. Mix in the brown sugar, white sugar, salt, spices, cinnamon, ground ginger, nutmeg, ground cloves, cardamom, and lemon zest.
3. Mix in the pumpkin purée. Stir in the cream. Beat together until everything is well mixed. Add cream to pumpkin pie puree
4. Pour the filling into an uncooked chilled or frozen pie shell. Bake at a high temperature of 425°F for 15 minutes.
5. Then after 15 minutes, lower the temperature to 350°F. Bake for 45 to 55 minutes more. The pie is done when a knife tip inserted in the center comes out wet but relatively clean. The center should be just barely jiggly.

Serving Suggestion: Serve with whipped cream.
Variation Tip: Add your favorite spices for variations.
Nutritional Information per Serving:
Calories 228.7|Carbohydrates 36.9g|Protein 6.4g|Fat 6.6g|Sodium 471.8mg|Fiber 0.9g

Giants' Rock Cakes

Prep Time: 15 minutes|Cook Time: 20 minutes|Servings: 12

Ingredients:

½ cup butter, cubed
1 cup white sugar
1 cup milk
3 cups plain flour, sifted

½ cup raisins
1 teaspoon baking powder
½ teaspoon vanilla extract

Preparation:

1. Preheat the oven to 325°F.
2. Mix the flour, sugar, and baking powder in a large bowl.
3. Next, using clean hands, blend the butter into the flour mixture until well incorporated and the mixture is crumbly.
4. Pour in the milk and whisk in the vanilla extract and raisins.
5. If necessary, gradually add more flour until you have a stiff dough.
6. Drop large tablespoons of the dough onto an oiled or parchment-lined baking sheet.
7. Bake until golden brown (around 20–30 minutes, depending on your oven).
8. Serve and enjoy!

Serving Suggestions: Serve with whipped cream on top.
Variation Tip: You can also add chocolate chips.
Nutritional Information per Serving:
Calories: 274|Fat: 8g|Sat Fat: 5g|Carbohydrates: 46g|Fiber: 1g|Sugar:21g|Protein: 4g

Canary Creams

Prep Time: 25 minutes|Cook Time: 35 minutes|Servings: 9

Ingredients

For the biscuits

2 cups almond flour	softened
1 tablespoon arrowroot flour	zest of 1 lemon
½ cup stevia	1 teaspoon vanilla extract
5 tablespoons unsalted butter,	¼ teaspoon sea salt

For the butter cream filling

2 ounces cream cheese, softened	3 to 4 drops yellow food coloring
4 tablespoons unsalted butter, softened	black decorative icing, chocolate mini chips, or sprinkles
6 tablespoons raw stevia	
1 tablespoon lemon juice	

Preparations

For the biscuits:

1. Mix all the
2. Ingredients in a food processor or by hand in a mixing bowl until the dough forms properly.
3. Place the dough in the refrigerator for a minimum of 30 minutes.
4. Preheat oven to 350°F. Line a baking tray with parchment paper.
5. Roll the chilled dough between two sheets of parchment paper with a rolling pin, roll the dough ½ inches thick. Cut into desired shapes. Bake for 10 to 15 minutes, or until the bread is lightly golden. Allow to cool. These beauties are delicate.

For the butter cream filling:

1. Cream the cream cheese, butter, stevia, and lemon juice, together with a hand mixer until fluffy.
2. Fill a piping bag with a fine tip to pipe. Pipe the butter cream evenly over the 9 biscuits. Then gently lay the 9 biscuits over the top.
3. Serve immediately and store leftovers in the refrigerator.

Serving Suggestion: Serve immediately along with chocolate milk.
Variation Tip: Add chocolate chips for chocolaty fun.
Nutritional Information Per Serving:
Calories 147|Carbohydrates 22g|Protein 1g|Fat 6g|Sodium 48mg|Fiber 2g

Choco Frogs

Prep Time: 10 minutes|Cook Time: 0 minutes|Servings: 12

Ingredients:

4 cups chocolate, melted	Frog-shaped chocolate molds

Preparation:

1. Pour the melted chocolate into the ungreased chocolate molds. Hit the molds against a hard surface several times to level out the chocolate and remove any air bubbles.
2. Place the molds in the freezer for at least 5 minutes. Remove the molds from the freezer, flip them over, and smack them against a clean surface until the chocolates fall out.
3. Serve and enjoy!

Serving Suggestions: Serve on top of ice cream.
Variation Tip: You can use any chocolate you prefer.
Nutritional Information per Serving:
Calories: 300|Fat: 16g|Sat Fat: 11g|Carbohydrates: 33g|Fiber: 1g|Sugar: 28g|Protein: 5g

Chocolate Rock Cakes

Prep Time: 10 minutes|Cook Time: 30 minutes|Servings: 2

Ingredients

For sponge cake:

1 cup flour	½ cup sugar
1 teaspoon baking powder	3 eggs, room temperature
a pinch of salt	2 tablespoons cocoa powder
8 tablespoons butter, room temperature	½ cup confectioner's sugar, for dusting

For custard filling:

½ cup whole milk	a pinch of salt
¼ cup heavy cream	2 egg yolks
½ cup sugar, divided	1 teaspoon vanilla
1½ tablespoons corn starch	

Preparation

1. Preheat the oven to 350°F and grease two ramekins.
2. In a small bowl, mix together the flour, baking powder, and salt. Beat together the sugar, butter, and eggs until light and fluffy in a separate bowl.
3. Slowly add the dry
4. Ingredients to the batter and add the cocoa powder. Stir until completely incorporated.
5. Put into the oven for 25 to 30 minutes, or until the tops are brown and a toothpick inserted in the center comes out clean.
6. Let the cakes rest in the ramekins for 10 minutes before tipping out onto a rack to cool completely.
7. While the cakes are cooling, use a sauce pan over medium-low heat to bring the milk, sugar, vanilla extract, and cornstarch to a simmer.
8. Add the yolks with a tablespoon of the milk mix before adding to the pan. Whisk constantly to keep the eggs from scrambling. Remove from the heat and continue to stir until

the custard is smooth and creamy.
9. Spread the custard onto the tops of one of the cakes and use the other cake to make a sandwich.

Serving Suggestion: Garnish with confectioner's sugar, serve with a mug of milk.
Variation Tip: Add chocolate chips for crunch.
Nutritional Information Per Serving:
Calories 166.6|Carbohydrates 26.1g|Protein 2.5g|Fat 5.6g|Sodium 96.9mg|Fiber 1g

Creamy Chocolate Gateau

Prep Time: 30 minutes|Cook Time: 20 minutes|Servings: 18

Ingredients:

2 boxes premix cake	2 ounces bittersweet chocolate, melted
1 cup heavy cream	
¼ cup confectioners' sugar	½ cup chopped, toasted pecans for decoration
1 teaspoon vanilla extract	

Preparation:

1. Bake 2 chocolate cake as per given direction of package at 350°F .
2. Combine the heavy cream, sugar and vanilla in a large mixing bowl and beat until stiff peaks form. Whisk ¼ cup of the whipped cream into the chocolate to lighten it. Then fold the rest of the whipped cream into the melted chocolate.
3. To assemble the gateau, place 1 cake layer on a platter. Spread ½ of the chocolate whipped cream over the cake layer, then ½ of the chocolate pastry cream over the whipped cream.
4. Repeat with another cake layer. Top with the last cake layer. Spread the glaze over the top layer and sprinkle the chopped pecans on top.

Serving Suggestion: Serve along with ice cream.
Variation Tip: Add nuts of your choice.
Nutritional Information per Serving:
Calories 451.3|Carbohydrates 37.9g|Protein 6.2g|Fat 33.1g|Sodium 75.9mg|Fiber 2.7g

Birthday Cake Biscotti

Prep Time: 10 minutes|Cook Time: 55 minutes|Servings: 12

Ingredients

3½ cups of flour
1 teaspoon of baking powder
¾ teaspoon kosher salt
1 cup oil
1 cup sugar
3 eggs
1 tablespoon vanilla extract
½ teaspoon butter
¼ cup of black sprinkles
¼ cup of green sprinkles
parchment paper
biscotti wrappers, as you like

Preparation

1. Preheat your oven to 350°F and line a large baking sheet with parchment paper.
2. In a large bowl, mix thoroughly your flour, baking powder, and kosher salt.
3. In another large bowl, mix your oil, sugar, eggs, vanilla, and imitation butter.
4. Once blended, slowly add your flour mixture until both the dry and wet mixtures are combined to make thick dough.
5. Mix sprinkles into the dough. Form dough logs that are 4 to 5 inches wide on your baking pans, making sure to leave space between the logs if you are placing multiple logs on one pan.
6. Sprinkle the top of your dough with a little extra salt and sugar.
7. Bake at 350°F for 25 minutes, then remove your pans from the oven.
8. Let your dough cool slightly; then, using a serrated knife, slice your biscotti into pieces that are about 1½ to 2 inches thick.
9. Reduce the temperature to 250°F.
10. While your oven adjusts the temperature, arrange your biscotti pieces on their side on your pans.
11. Place them back in the oven to cook for 20 to 30 more minutes at the lower temperature.

Serving Suggestion: Serve with coffee or tea.
Variation Tip: Add nuts for an extra crunch.
Nutritional Information Per Serving:
Calories 513|Carbohydrates 63g|Protein 9g|Fat 25g|Sodium 56mg|Fiber 1g

Enchanting Blueberry Lavender Pie

Prep Time: 25 minutes|Cook Time: 1 hour|Servings: 8

Ingredients

2 pie crust rounds, chilled
6 cups fresh blueberries
½ cup plus 2 tablespoons granulated sugar
3 to 4 tablespoons cornstarch
2 teaspoons dried lavender
1 tablespoon lemon juice
2 teaspoons vanilla extract
1 tablespoon cold salted butter, cut into small pieces
1 egg, beaten

Preparation

1. Fit 1 pie crust round into a 9-inch pie plate. Lightly prick the bottom of the dough with a fork. In a large bowl, toss together the blueberries, ½ cup of sugar, cornstarch, 2 teaspoons of lavender, lemon juice, and vanilla. Pour the berries into the crust. Arrange the butter pieces evenly over the berries.
2. Grab the second pie crust round and roll it out into a 12-inch circle. Place the crust over the berries. Alternately you can create a lattice design if desired. Using a fork, crimp the edges of the crust together to seal the pie up.
3. In a bowl, combine 2 tablespoons of sugar with 1 teaspoon of lavender. Pinch the lavender and sugar together with your fingers to break the buds up into the sugar.
4. Brush the top crust with the beaten egg and sprinkle with lavender sugar.
5. Slice four holes in the top of the crust for air pockets. Cover and chill pie until crust is firm, 1 hour in the fridge or 30 minutes in the freezer.
6. Preheat the oven to 400°F. Bake for 20 minutes, and then reduce the oven to 350°F and bake for another 30 minutes until the pie is golden and the sauce is bubbling.

Serving Suggestion: Serve warm topped with ice cream.
Variation Tip: Add berries of your choice.
Nutritional Information Per Serving:
Calories 410|Carbohydrates 37g|Protein 9g|Fat 26g|Sodium 205mg|Fiber 2g

Cauldron Cake

Prep Time: 10 minutes|Cook Time: 30 minutes|Servings: 2

Ingredients

¼ cup flour	2 tablespoons buttermilk
¼ teaspoon salt	1 egg
¼ teaspoon baking powder	¼ teaspoon vanilla
¼ teaspoon baking soda	2 cups French butter cream
3 tablespoons cocoa powder	frosting
¼ cup sugar	¼ teaspoon red food gel
2 tablespoons vegetable oil	¼ teaspoon yellow food gel

Preparation

1. Preheat the oven to 375˚F.
2. In a small bowl, whisk together the dry
3. Ingredients then add the wet
4. Ingredients and stir until smooth.
5. Make sure to beat out all the chunks until you get a smooth but thick batter.
6. Pour the batter into the cauldron cake tin until ⅔-full. Do not overfill.
7. Place them on a baking sheet to catch any spills that may happen.
8. Bake for 28 to 30 minutes, until a toothpick inserted in the center comes out clean.
9. Let the cake cool to room temperature then chill while preparing the butter cream.
10. If you have made plain white butter cream frosting, use the food gels to color the frosting. Place the frosting in the center of a 15-inch-by-15-inch-square plastic wrap and roll into a tube. Place both wrapped frostings into a piping bag with a star or drop tip.
11. Pipe the frosting in multiple layers to recreate the flames on top of the cauldron cake.

Serving Suggestion: Serve chilled and enjoy.
Variation Tip: Use butterscotch candy chunks for a crunch.
Nutritional Information Per Serving:
Calories 150|Carbohydrates 19g|Protein 1g|Fat 9g|Sodium 30mg|Fiber 1g

Choco Clusters

Prep Time: 10 minutes|Cook Time: 0 minutes|Servings: 12

Ingredients:

½ cup chocolate chips	1½ cups dry chow mein
¼ cup butterscotch chips	noodles

Preparation:

1. Microwave the chocolate and butterscotch chips together in a bowl, stirring until smooth.
2. Coat the dry chow mein noodles evenly in the mixture.
3. Drop a tablespoon of noodles on a baking sheet lined with wax paper to form little "nests."
4. Allow them to cool completely before serving.
5. Serve and enjoy!

Serving Suggestions: Garnish with sprinkles on top.
Variation Tip: You can use mini pretzels instead if you prefer.
Nutritional Information per Serving:
Calories: 67|Fat: 3g|Sat Fat: 1g|Carbohydrates: 7g|Fiber: 0.5g|Sugar: 5g|Protein: 1g

Treacle Tart

Prep Time: 10 minutes|Cook Time: 25 minutes|Servings: 8

Ingredients

1 cup light corn syrup
⅓ cup black treacle
2 cups plain bread crumbs
1 lemon, juiced & zested
1 pie pastry crust
1 tablespoon water + 1 egg, whisked
Whipped cream, for topping

Preparation

1. In a large bowl, microwave 1 to 3 cups water until it is steaming hot but not boiling.
2. Place a smaller bowl in the center of the larger bowl so that the water comes about half way up the sides. Pour the golden syrup into the bowl along with the black treacle. Let it soften for about ten minutes.
3. Preheat the oven to 375°F.
4. Stir the breadcrumbs into the softened syrups still in the bowl. Stir in the lemon juice and zest. Let it rest another five minutes.
5. Prepare the pie crust by gently pressing the crust into a fluted pie pan or tart dish.
6. Spoon the filling into the center and press down to fill any pockets. Fold the excess dough over the edges of the filling or prepare a weave for the top of the tart.
7. Whisk together the egg and water and generously brush over the entire top of the filling and any overlapping dough.
8. Bake for 20 to 25 minutes, until the crust is golden brown and the tart has set in the center.

Serving Suggestion: Serve warm topped with whipped cream.
Variation Tip: Serve with your favorite ice cream.
Nutritional Information Per Serving:
Calories 382|Carbohydrates 59.2g|Protein 3.8g|Fat 15.9g|Sodium 0.6g|Fiber 1g

Sleep You Draft Cupcakes

Prep Time: 10 minutes|Cook Time: 30 minutes|Servings: 12

Ingredients

1¾ cups flour
1½ teaspoons baking powder
½ teaspoon salt
½ cup unsalted butter, zest of 1 lemon
½ lemon juice
¼ teaspoon freshly ground nutmeg
¾ cup milk
2 eggs
¾ cup high quality honey +
¼ cup honey for drizzling on top
1 teaspoon vanilla
chocolate (garnishing)

Preparations

1. Preheat the oven to 350°F.
2. Line the cupcake tray.
3. In a medium bowl, whisk together the flour, baking powder, salt, nutmeg and lemon zest.
4. Mix in the room temperature butter to the flour mixture until it looks like a crumbly mixture. Set aside.
5. In a small bowl, whisk together the milk, eggs, honey, and vanilla.
6. Pour the liquids over the dry mixture and combine until just combined.
7. Spoon the batter into cupcake lining about ⅓-full each.
8. Bake for 16 minutes until the toothpick test comes out clean. Cool the cakes on the racks.
9. For sleep you draft: Warm the remaining ¼ cup of honey in the microwave for about 10 seconds with ½ teaspoon of lemon juice. Mix well.
10. Using a pastry brush, coat the tops of the cakes with the honey. Allow to sit for about 5 minutes to let the honey soak into the cakes.
11. Melt the chocolate in the microwave and spread over the top in form of disc.

Serving Suggestion: Serve and enjoy.
Variation Tip: Use butterscotch candy chunks for crunch.
Nutritional Information Per Serving:
Calories 180|Carbohydrates 39g|Protein 4g|Fat 2g|Sodium 33mg|Fiber 1g

Monster Cake

Prep Time: 35 minutes | Cook Time: 30 minutes | Servings: 16 slices

Ingredients
Cake
6 eggs
1½ cups sugar
1¼ cups buttermilk

1¼ cups rapeseed oil
3⅔ cups cake flour
4½ teaspoons baking powder

Filling
2 cups milk
1 packet vanilla pudding powder
¼ cup sugar

vanilla extract to taste
1¼ cups unsalted butter
black currant jam

Chocolate frosting
½ cup unsalted butter at room temperature
1¾ cups icing sugar
¼ cup unsweetened cocoa

powder
¼ teaspoon salt
vanilla extract to taste
1 to 2 tablespoons milk

Decoration
1 small piece of pink fondant
1 small piece of blue fondant
some shortening

4 round chocolate bonbons
1 teaspoon unsweetened cocoa powder

Preparations
Pudding
1. Prepare the pudding well in advance as it will need several hours to reach room temperature. Measure the 2 cups of milk in a pot.
2. Remove about 6 tablespoons of the milk from this amount and place it into a small bowl. Place the pot with the milk on the heat and slowly bring to a boil.
3. In the meantime, whisk the remaining milk with the sugar and the pudding powder. When the milk comes to a boil, slowly pour the pudding mixture into the hot milk while whisking continuously.
4. Let a few bubbles appear once or twice and then remove from heat. Place a piece of cling film over the pot and let the pudding come to room temperature, preferably overnight.

Cake
1. Preheat the oven to 320°F. Line two 12-by-15-inch baking trays with baking paper.
2. Beat the eggs and the sugar well until light and fluffy. Add the buttermilk and the oil to the mixture slowly while mixing.
3. Mix the flour and baking powder together and sift them over the egg mixture. Mix well.
4. Divide the mixture between the prepared baking trays and bake for about 15 to 20 minutes or until golden. Let cool completely.

Butter cream
1. To make the butter cream both butter and vanilla pudding should be at room temperature. Mix the butter until very light and fluffy.
2. Start adding the vanilla pudding to the butter one tablespoon at a time, only adding the next tablespoon when the one before it is completely incorporated. Add vanilla extract to taste.

Filling
1. Cut each cake into two equal parts. Trim the edges of the cake and make sure they have exactly the same size.
2. Place one cake layer on a board or a rectangular serving platter.
3. Keep ⅓ of the vanilla butter cream for covering the edges of the cake.
4. Cover the first cake layer with half of the jam and some butter cream. Cover with a second layer of cake and only with butter cream.
5. Place the third cake layer on top and cover it with the remaining jam and with butter cream. Place the last layer on top and press lightly to stabilize the cake.
6. Use about half of the remaining vanilla butter cream to thinly cover the edges of the cake. (There is no need to cover the top of the monster cake with butter cream, as you will pipe the chocolate frosting on top.)
7. Place the cake in the refrigerator for about half an hour or until set. In the meantime, prepare the chocolate frosting, the tongue, and the eyes of the monster.

Frosting
1. Cream the butter for a few minutes in a mixer. Stop the mixer and sift in the icing sugar, the unsweetened cocoa powder, and the salt on top of the butter.
2. Continue mixing on the lowest speed at first until the

icing sugar is incorporated. Add vanilla extract.

3. Add 1 tablespoon of the milk and mix the frosting on medium-high speed for about 3 minutes. If the mixture seems stiff for piping, you can add the second tablespoon of milk. Place the frosting in a piping bag fitted with the grass piping tip.

Tongue and eyes

1. Knead the pink fondant with a little shortening until pliable. Roll it thinly on a smooth surface and cut a long stripe about 5 inches long and 1.4 inches wide. Cut the tip of the tongue to resemble a snake's tongue.
2. Knead and thinly roll the blue fondant as well. Cut out four very small rounds, paint them black for the pupils.

Assemble

1. Take the cake out of the fridge. Use the remaining vanilla butter cream to cover the edges of the cake with a second layer of butter cream.
2. Lightly brush the pages of the book with the cocoa powder to give the book an old, battered look.
3. Place the tongue on the cake.
4. Pipe the chocolate frosting on the cake, going around the edges first and filling the top of the cake. Pipe some chocolate frosting at the base of the cake and the board.
5. Only pipe the back of the cake with frosting when the cake is completely finished.
6. Place the eyes on the cake. Pipe some more frosting around the eyes to give them a bushy look.

Serving Suggestion: Cut in slices and serve chilled with the butter beer.
Variation Tip: Pipe the leftover frosting on the back of the cake, if you wish.
Nutritional Information Per Serving:
Calories 540|Carbohydrates 207mg|Protein 6g|Fat 34g|Sodium 104mg|Fiber 1g

Apple Strudel

Prep Time: 10 minutes|Cook Time: 35 minutes|Servings: 4

Ingredients

2 sheets puff pastries, thawed	¼ cup flour
2 red apples, cored & sliced thin	¼ cup sugar
	1 tablespoon cinnamon
4 tablespoons raisins	½ teaspoon salt
2 tablespoons lemon juice	1 tablespoon water + 1 egg, whisked

Preparation

1. Preheat the oven to 350°F.
2. Wash and core the apples, then slice thinly. Place the sliced apples in a bowl and toss with the lemon juice, raisins, sea salt, flour, sugar and cinnamon.
3. Let it rest for about five to ten minutes to let the flour absorb as much of the moisture as possible. Stir occasionally.
4. Unfold the thawed puff pastries. On a lightly floured surface, use a rolling pin to press together the seams and roll out the pastries to consistent thickness.
5. Arrange the apple slices down the center of each pastry, leaving the sides open and about 1 to 2 inches of the dough at the top and bottom.
6. Evenly distribute the apple slices in an overlapping row on each pastry. Top with raisins from the flour mixture. Sprinkle any remaining flour/sugar from the bowl onto the tops of the apples.
7. Use a sharp knife to cut to about a half inch away from the apples. Cut ½-inch-thick slices down each open side of the pastry.
8. Fold the top and bottom over the apples. In an alternating pattern, cross one strip of dough over the apples, then take the same strip from the other side and cross it over the first, forming a "V" or "X" like shape. Repeat with every strip, folding the last over the dough on the bottom and tucking under the pasty.
9. Transfer the pastries to a parchment lined baking sheet. Whisk together one egg with a tablespoon of water.
10. Brush the pastries with the egg wash and bake for 30 to 35 minutes, until golden brown and fragrant.

Serving Suggestion: Serve warm.
Variation Tip: Sprinkle icing sugar on top for a velvety touch.
Nutritional Information Per Serving:
Calories 194|Carbohydrates 29.2g|Protein 2.3g|Fat 8g|Sodium 191mg|Fiber 1.6g

Enchanted Povitica

Prep Time: 40 minutes|Cook Time: 1 hour|Servings: 4 loaves

Ingredients:

To activate the Yeast:

2 teaspoons sugar	½ cup warm water
1 teaspoon all-purpose flour	2 tablespoons dry yeast

Dough:

2 cups whole milk	½ cup unsalted butter, melted
¾ cup sugar	8 cups sifted all-purpose
3 teaspoons table salt	flour, divided
4 large eggs	

Topping:

½ cup cold strong coffee	sugar
2 tablespoons granulated	Melted butter

Walnut Filling:

7 cups ground English	1 teaspoon vanilla extract
walnuts	2 cups granulated sugar
1 cup whole milk	1 teaspoon unsweetened
1 cup unsalted butter	cocoa powder
2 whole eggs, beaten	1 teaspoon cinnamon

Preparation:

1. Make Walnut Filling: In a large bowl mix together ground walnuts, sugar, cinnamon, and cocoa.

2. Heat milk and butter to boiling. Pour the liquid over the nut sugar mixture. Add eggs and vanilla and mix thoroughly.

3. Allow the filling to stand at room temperature until ready to be spread onto the dough. If the mixture thickens, stir in a small amount of warm milk.

4. Activate Yeast: In a small bowl, stir 2 teaspoons sugar, 1 teaspoon flour, and the yeast into warm water and cover with plastic wrap. Allow yeast to stand for 5 minutes.

5. Make the Dough: In a medium saucepan, heat the milk up to just below boiling, stirring constantly so that a film does not form on the top of the milk. Cool slightly, until it is about 110°F.

6. In a large bowl, mix the scalded milk, ¾ cup sugar, and the salt until combined.

7. Add the beaten eggs, yeast mixture, melted butter, and 2 cups of flour.

8. Blend thoroughly and slowly add remaining flour, mixing well until the dough just starts to clean the bowl.

9. Don't add too much flour at this point; you still want it to be fairly wet and sticky. Turn dough out onto a floured surface and knead, gradually adding flour a little at a time, until smooth and does not stick.

10. Divide the dough into 4 equal pieces .Place dough in 4 lightly oiled bowls, cover loosely with a layer of plastic wrap and then a kitchen towel and let rise in a warm place for an hour and a half, or until doubled in size.

11. To Roll and Assemble the Dough: Spread a clean sheet or cloth over your entire table so that it is covered. Sprinkle sheet with a couple of tablespoons, to a handful of flour.

12. Place the dough on the sheet and roll the dough out with a rolling pin, starting in the middle and working your way out, until it measures roughly 10-12 inches in diameter. Spoon 1 to 1.5 teaspoon of melted butter on top.

13. Using the tops of your hands, stretch the dough out from the center until the dough is thin and uniformly opaque. If you prefer, you can use a rolling pin. As you work, continually pick up the dough from the table, not only to help in stretching it out but also to make sure that it isn't sticking. When you think it the dough is thin enough, try to get it a little thinner. It should be so thin that you can see the color and perhaps the pattern on the sheet underneath.

14. Spoon filling evenly over the dough until covered. Lift the edge of the cloth and gently roll the dough up like a jelly roll. Once the dough is rolled up into a log shape, gently lift it up and place it in the shape of a U into a greased loaf pan, with the ends meeting in the middle. You want to coil the dough around itself, as this will give the dough its characteristic look when sliced. Repeat with remaining three loaves.

15. Brush the top of each loaf with a mixture of ½ cup of cold strong coffee and 2 tablespoons of sugar. If you prefer, you can use egg whites in place of the coffee.

16. Cover pans lightly with plastic wrap and allow to rest for approximately 15 minutes.

17. Meanwhile, preheat oven to 350°F. Remove plastic wrap from dough and place into the preheated oven and

bake for approximately 15 minutes. Turn down the oven temperature to 300°F. and bake for an additional 45 minutes, or until done. Check the Povitica every 30 minutes to ensure that the bread is not getting too brown. You may cover the loaves with a sheet of aluminum foil if you need to.

18. Remove bread from the oven, brush with melted butter, then allow to cool on a wire rack for 20-30 minutes.

19. The best ways to cut Povitica loaves into slices is by turning the loaf upside down and slice with a serrated knife.

Serving Suggestion: Serve warm with hot chocolate.
Variation Tip: Use almonds as a filling.
Nutritional Information per Serving:
Calories 296|Carbohydrates 31g|Protein 6g|Fat 17g|Sodium 152mg|Fiber 2g

Butter Beer Caramel Cake

Prep Time: 1 hour|Cook Time: 30 minutes|Servings: 1 9-inch cake

Ingredients

Butter beer cake

2 cups cake flour	sugar blend, packed
1½ teaspoons baking powder	3 large eggs, room
½ teaspoon baking soda	temperature
½ teaspoon salt	1 cup buttermilk
½ cup unsalted butter,	2 teaspoons vanilla extract
softened	2 teaspoons butter flavouring
¾ cup brown sugar or brown	caramel syrup

Brown butter vanilla frosting

¼ cup butter, and ½ cup	½ cup powdered sugar
butter	¼ cup brown sugar
3 tablespoon flour	1 batch salted butterscotch
¾ cup whole milk	ganache
1½ teaspoons vanilla extract	

Preparation

Butter beer cake:

1. Preheat oven to 350°F. Line pan with parchment, then grease and flour it.

2. In a bowl, mix the flour, baking soda, baking powder, and salt until combined. Add the sugar and mix.

3. Add the softened butter to the mixture and mix until the texture is crumbly.

4. In a separate bowl, mix the eggs, vanilla, butter flavoring, and caramel syrup. Slowly add it to the flour mixture and mix until combined. Slowly incorporate the buttermilk until smooth.

5. Add the batter to a 9-inch cake pan and bake for 25 to 28 minutes, testing the middle with a cake tester or a toothpick.

6. Once the cake is done, let cool in the pan for 10 minutes. Remove the cake and let it cool completely on a wire rack.

7. Level the cake with a knife as needed

Brown butter vanilla frosting:

1. Brown ¼ cup of butter on medium-high heat and then add flour and whisk together.

2. Slowly whisk in the milk, working out any lumps. Keep whisking while bringing the mixture to a boil so it thickens.

3. Once boiled, whisk in the vanilla extract and remove the mixture and let it cool.

4. While the mixture is cooling, cream together the ½ cup of butter with sugars.

5. Once the flour mixture is completely cool, beat it into the mixing bowl with the sugar mixture. Cream both mixtures together until fluffy.

To assemble:

1. Put a dab of frosting on your cake plate, and then add one layer of cake. Spread frosting over the top of the cake as thick as you like, and then drizzle the butterscotch sauce over the frosting. Repeat with as many layers as you have.

2. On the last layer of cake, spread frosting over the top and sides and smooth around the edges and top.

3. Drizzle more butterscotch sauce over the top of the cake, just enough to cover the top and let some drizzle down the sides.

Serving Suggestion: Slice the cake and serve.
Variation Tip: Add any decorations you like such as butterscotch chips or fondant golden snitches.
Nutritional Information Per Serving:
Calories 253.7|Carbohydrates 50g|Protein 1.2g|Fat 6.8g|Sodium 173.9mg|Fiber 0.4g

Owl Cupcakes

Prep Time: 30 minutes | Cook Time: 15 minutes | Servings: 12

Ingredients

Cupcakes

2 cups white sugar
2 cups all-purpose flour, sifted
1 cup unsweetened cocoa powder
2 teaspoons baking powder
1 teaspoon salt
½ teaspoon baking soda
1 cup buttermilk
½ cup vegetable oil
2 eggs
1 teaspoon vanilla extract
1 cup hot water

Frosting

¾ cup heavy whipping cream
1½ tablespoons heavy whipping cream
1½ cups mascarpone cheese
2 tablespoons mascarpone cheese
7 tablespoons unsweetened cocoa powder
¼ cup white sugar

Decoration

48 chocolate sandwich cookies
48 brown candy-coated milk chocolate pieces
24 oranges or yellow candy-coated milk chocolate pieces
fondant for wings and body (yellow, blue, green, pink and purple)

Preparation

1. Preheat oven to 350°F. Line 2 muffin tins.
2. Combine the sugar, flour, cocoa powder, baking powder, salt, and baking soda in a bowl. Whisk buttermilk, vegetable oil, eggs, and vanilla extract in a large bowl. Add flour mixture, mix until well-combined.
3. Pour in hot water, stir until batter is smooth. Divide batter evenly among the muffin tins.
4. Bake in the preheated oven about 12 minutes. Transfer cupcakes to a wire rack and let them cool completely, about 20 minutes.
5. Whip ¾ cup plus 1½ tablespoons of heavy cream in a bowl with an electric mixer until soft peaks formed.
6. Gently fold in 1½ cups plus 2 tablespoons of mascarpone cheese, 7 tablespoons of cocoa powder, and ¼ cup of sugar gently to make frosting.
7. Spread 1 tablespoon of frosting over each cooled cupcake.
8. Twist chocolate sandwich cookies open, leaving all cream filling on 1 side.
9. Place 2 cookies, cream filling side up, on each cupcake to make owl eyes.
10. Place a brown milk chocolate piece on each cookie to create pupils.
11. Insert an orange or yellow milk chocolate piece in the centre to make a beak.
12. Spread the fondant with the rolling pin and cut the wings and body of the owls with knife or the shape cutter.
13. Flatten the orange/yellow fondant and cut the little angles for beak and toes.
14. Centre the body under the eyes top on the frosted cake. Adjust wings on side. Carefully manage beak and toes and gently press them for adjustment. Use little water with brush if you find difficulty to place beak and toe on the fondant belly.
15. Repeat the process with all the cupcakes.

Serving Suggestion: Serve at a Halloween party.
Variation Tip: Use butter beer ganache as a filling in the cupcakes, or use other kind of vegetables or fruit sauce to make colorful and tasteful cupcakes.
Nutritional Information Per Serving:
Calories 372 | Carbohydrates 46.4g | Protein 5.4g | Fat 20.3g | Sodium 291.3mg | Fiber 2.1g

Furr's Chocolate Sheet Cake

Prep Time: 20 minutes | Cook Time: 20 minutes | Servings: 24

Ingredients:

For the Cake:

2 cups flour	1 cup boiling water
2 cups sugar	½ cup buttermilk
¼ teaspoon salt	2 whole beaten eggs
4 tablespoons cocoa	1 teaspoon baking soda
2 sticks butter	1 teaspoon vanilla

For the Frosting:

½ cup finely chopped pecans	6 tablespoons milk
1 ¾ stick butter	1 teaspoon vanilla
4 tablespoons cocoa	1 pound powdered sugar

Preparation:

1. In a mixing bowl, combine flour, sugar, and salt. In a saucepan, melt butter. Add cocoa. Stir together.

2. Add boiling water, allow mixture to boil for 30 seconds, then turn off heat. Pour over flour mixture, and stir lightly to cool.

3. In a measuring cup, pour the buttermilk and add beaten eggs, baking soda, and vanilla. Stir buttermilk mixture into butter/chocolate mixture.

4. Pour into sheet cake pan and bake at 350°F for 20 minutes.

5. While cake is baking, make the icing. Chop pecans finely. Melt butter in a saucepan. Add cocoa, stir to combine, and then turn off heat. Add the milk, vanilla, and powdered sugar. Stir together. Add the pecans, stir together, and pour over warm cake.

6. Cut into squares, eat, and totally wig out over the fact that you've just made the best chocolate sheet cake. Ever.

7. First, melt 2 sticks regular butter in a saucepan. While it's melting, boil 1 cup of water.

8. When the butter is melted, add 4 heaping tablespoons cocoa powder and mix thoroughly.

9. With the heat still on, pour in the boiling water.

10. And allow the mixture to bubble for 30 seconds. Turn off heat. Set aside.

11. In a large mixing bowl, combine 2 cups flour, 2 cups sugar and ¼ tsp salt .Stir together.

12. Pour the hot butter and chocolate mixture over the top and stir together slightly, just to cool the chocolate.

13. In a measuring cup, pour ½ cup buttermilk.

14. To the buttermilk, add 2 beaten eggs, 1 teaspoon vanilla, and 1 teaspoon baking soda. Stir together.

15. Add the buttermilk mixture to the chocolate/flour mixture. Stir together well.

16. Pour the luscious batter into the ungreased pan and spread it evenly.

17. Bake the cake at 350°F for 20 minutes. While the cake is baking, it's time to make the evil, decadent frosting.

18. Chop ½ cup pecans into pretty small pieces.

19. In a saucepan, melt 1 ¾ sticks of regular butter .Once the butter is melted, add 4 heaping tablespoons cocoa powder.

20. Stir together, and allow to bubble for 30 seconds. Turn off heat. Then add 6 tablespoons milk and 1 teaspoon vanilla. Stir together.

21. Then add 1 pound of powdered sugar. Stir together then add the chopped pecans and stir together again.

22. Now pour the evil, adulterous, wicked frosting over the warm, ridiculous cake.

23. Try to pour it all over the surface, so you won't have to do much spreading.

24. The warmth of the cake should do most of the work for you, causing the stupidly delicious frosting to spread on its own. You'll have to help it along a little, but the less you have to spread, the better.

Serving Suggestion: Serve cold with yummy topping.

Variation Tip: Add your favorite chopped nut and make sure chop them very finely. It will be much crunchier.

Nutritional Information per Serving:

Calories 314|Carbohydrates 42.6g|Protein 2.5g|Fat 15.7g|Sodium 138.3mg|Fiber 0.7g

Ronald's Sponge Sandwich Cake

Prep Time: 30 minutes|Cook Time: 20 minutes|Servings: 18

Ingredients:

1.5 cups all-purpose flour	1 cup granulated sugar
1 teaspoon baking powder	3 large eggs, at room
¼ teaspoon salt	temperature
12 teaspoon butter, at room	Confectioner's sugar, for
temperature	dusting

For the Custard Filling:

1 cup whole milk plus ½ cup	Pinch of salt
heavy cream	3 large egg yolks
¼ cup granulated sugar,	½ teaspoon vanilla extract
divided	1 tablespoon butter
3 tablespoons cornstarch	Whipped cream, for serving

Preparation:

1. Preheat the oven to 350°F. Grease two 8" cake pans and line the bottoms with parchment paper.

2. Whisk together the flour, baking powder, and salt in a mixing bowl and set aside.

3. Using an electric mixer, beat the butter and sugar in a large bowl until light and fluffy, scraping down the sides as needed, about 5 minutes.

4. Add the eggs to the butter one at a time, beating after each until incorporated and scraping the sides as needed.

5. Add the flour mixture and mix on the slowest speed until combined. Finish by scraping down the sides and folding the batter together with a rubber spatula.

6. Divide the batter evenly between the two pans and bake for about 20 minutes until the cakes are golden brown around the edges and they feel soft but firm when touched in the center or a toothpick inserted comes out clean.

7. Let the cakes cool in the pans for 10 minutes, then invert onto a wire rack to cool completely.

8. To make the custard, combine the milk or milk and cream, 2 tablespoons of the sugar, cornstarch, and salt in a small saucepan and mix until the cornstarch is dissolved.

9. Whisk the yolks with the remaining sugar in a medium bowl until smooth.

10. Heat the milk mixture over medium-high heat, stirring constantly, until it is hot but not bubbling. Reduce the heat to low.

11. Temper the egg yolk mixture by pouring ½ cup of the hot milk into the yolks while whisking constantly. Pour the yolk mixture slowly back into the saucepan while stirring constantly.

12. Return the pan to medium-high heat, stirring constantly, until the mixture thickens and begins to boil.

13. Remove the pan from the heat and add the vanilla. Add the butter if you did not use heavy cream. Stir gently until combined .If you're picky about lumps, strain the custard through a sieve. Cover with plastic wrap and refrigerate until cold.

14. To assemble the cake, place one cake layer top-side down on your plate and spread the custard over the cake to within ½" of the cake's edge. Top with the other layer and dust with confectioner's sugar.

15. Keep the cake refrigerated, but bring to room temperature before serving. Serve with whipped cream.

Serving Suggestion: Serve with tea.

Variation Tip: Add chopped nut or chocolate ganache.

Nutritional Information per Serving:

Calories 325.2|Carbohydrates 49.2g|Protein 11.1g|Fat 12.3g|Sodium 287.2mg|Fiber 3.8g

Ganache Pudding

Prep Time: 15 minutes|Cook Time: 60 minutes|Servings: 20

Ingredients

Cake

1 cup unsalted butter	1 teaspoon salt
2½ cups caster sugar	3 cups milk
4 large eggs	1 cup vegetable oil
5 cups all-purpose flour	2 teaspoons vanilla extract
6 teaspoons baking powder	4 tablespoons Greek yogurt

Ganache

2¼ cups dark chocolate	1 cup heavy cream

Frosting

2 batches butter cream frosting	2 drops green food gel
	4 drops purple food gel

Decorations

20 maraschino cherries	12 purple candy flowers

Preparation

Ganache

1. Add the chocolate and heavy cream to a heat proof bowl and microwave for 30 seconds at a time, stirring each time until smooth. Allow to cool at room temperature.

Cake

1. Preheat the oven to 275°F. Spray a 10-inch and two 6-inch cake tins with oil spray and line the bottoms with baking paper. Set aside.

2. Add the flour, baking powder and salt to a large mixing bowl. Use a whisk to combine. Set aside.

3. Add the butter and sugar to a large mixing bowl and whip on high speed until light and fluffy. Add vanilla extract and the eggs one at a time, mixing and scraping the bowl down each time.

4. Add half of the dry

5. Ingredients in the bowl along with half of the milk. Stir with medium-low speed until well combined. Scrape down the bowl and add the remaining milk, dry

6. Ingredients, yogurt and oil. Stir with medium-low speed until well combined.

7. Distribute the batter evenly amongst the four baking tins, starting with the 10-inch baking tin first.

8. Bake for 50 to 60 minutes, or until a tooth pick inserted in the middle of the cake comes out clean. If the tooth pick is coated with wet batter, continue baking for 10 minutes at a time until fully baked. Allow the cakes to cool to room temperature in tins.

9. To crumb coat your cake, add a dab of chocolate ganache onto a 10-inch cake board or flat serving plate.

10. Use a small offset spatula to spread the frosting around before adding the first cake layer. Gently press down the centre of the cake layer to make sure it's stuck to the frosting underneath.

Decoration

1. Add ganache to a piping bag and frost a ring around the top of the cake. Fill the centre with more ganache.

2. Use a small offset spatula to smoothen out the frosting before you add the next layer of cake. Repeat with the remaining layers.

3. Cover the cake in a layer of ganache and spread around. Pipe a line of white butter cream around the bottom of the 10-inch cake, then again on the top of the 10-inch cake and two more up along the 6-inch cakes.

4. Pipe swirls of purple and green frosting in between the white frosting. Then finish with cherries on the bottom layer of swirls and some cherries on the top layer of swirls.

5. Add little purple flower candies on the bottom swirls in between the cherries.

Serving Suggestion: Serve with pumpkin beer.
Variation Tip: Use canned cherries as per taste.
Nutritional Information Per Serving:
Calories 482|Carbohydrates 38g|Protein 27g|Fat 34g|Sodium 271mg|Fiber 3g

Great Feast Apple Crumb Pie

Prep Time: 30 minutes|Cook Time: 2 hour +2 hour cooling time|Servings: 8

Ingredients:

For the Crust:

1 ¼ cups all-purpose flour, plus more for dusting

2 teaspoons granulated sugar

½ teaspoon salt

1 stick cold unsalted butter, cut into ½-inch cubes

1 tablespoon apple cider vinegar

¼ cup ice water, plus more if needed

For the Crumb Topping:

1 cup all-purpose flour

⅓ cup packed light brown sugar

¼ teaspoon ground cinnamon

¼ teaspoon salt

1 stick unsalted butter, cut into ½-inch pieces, at room temperature

For the Filling:

3 pounds mixed apples peeled and sliced ¼ inch thick

4 tablespoons unsalted butter, melted

⅓ cup granulated sugar

¼ cup packed light brown sugar

2 tablespoons all-purpose flour

1 tablespoon fresh lemon juice

1 teaspoon ground cinnamon

⅛ teaspoon salt

Preparation:

1. Make the crust: Whisk the flour, granulated sugar and salt in a large bowl. Rub the butter pieces into the flour using your fingers until pea-size pieces form.

2. Drizzle in the vinegar and ice water; stir gently with a fork to combine. If the dough doesn't hold together when you squeeze it, add more ice water, 1 tablespoon at a time.

3. Turn out the dough onto a piece of plastic wrap and form into a disk; wrap tightly. Refrigerate until firm, at least 1 hour or overnight.

4. Roll out the dough on a lightly floured surface into a 13-inch round. Ease into a 9-inch pie plate.

5. Trim the edges, leaving a 1-inch overhang, then tuck the overhanging dough under itself; crimp the edges with a fork. Refrigerate until firm, at least 1 hour or overnight.

6. The crumb topping: Mix the flour, brown sugar, cinnamon and salt in a medium bowl. Rub the butter into the mixture with your fingers until no longer floury and crumbs form. Freeze until ready to use.

7. Make the filling: Place a foil-lined baking sheet on the lowest oven rack; preheat to 400° F. Mix the apples, melted butter, sugars, flour, lemon juice, cinnamon and salt in a large bowl.

8. Spoon the filling into the chilled pie crust. Pat the crumb mixture on top.

9. Bake the pie on the hot baking sheet until lightly browned, about 30 minutes. Reduce the oven temperature to 350° F and bake until the apples are completely soft when pierced with a paring knife, 60 to 80 more minutes.

10. Transfer the pie to a rack to cool completely.

Serving Suggestion: Serve warm with butter beer ice-cream.

Variation Tip: Use butterscotch for flavor.

Nutritional Information per Serving:
Calories 373.7|Carbohydrates 60.3g|Protein 2.8g|Fat 14.8g|Sodium 51.4mg|Fiber 3 g

Apple Tart

Prep Time: 25 minutes|Cook Time: 50 minutes|Servings: 8

Ingredients:

1 cup sugar, divided	6 medium tart apples, peeled
2 tablespoons all-purpose	and thinly sliced
flour	1 tablespoon butter
½ teaspoon ground cinnamon	Pastry for a single-crust pie

Preparation:

1. In a 10-inches cast-iron or other ovenproof skillet, heat ¾ cup sugar, stirring constantly until it is liquefied and golden brown. Remove from the heat.

2. In a small bowl, combine the flour, cinnamon and remaining sugar. Arrange half the apples in a single layer in skillet. Sprinkle with half the sugar mixture. Arrange half the remaining apples in circular pattern over sugar; sprinkle with remaining sugar mixture. Place remaining apples over all, keeping the top as level as possible. Dot with butter.

3. Roll out dough to 11-in. circle; place over apples, pressing gently to completely cover. Do not flute.

4. Bake at 400°F until apples are tender and golden brown, about 50 minutes.

5. Cool 5 minutes before inverting onto a serving plate.

Serving Suggestion: Serve cold topped with butter beer ice cream.

Variation Tip: Use butterscotch candy chunks for crunch.

Nutritional Information per Serving:

Calories 284|Carbohydrates 52g|Protein 1g|Fat 9g|Sodium 115mg|Fiber 2g

Kentucky Derby Pie Bread Pudding

Prep Time: 30 minutes|Cook Time: 2 hour|Servings: 18

Ingredients:

2 tablespoons vanilla extract	1 ½ cups pecans, chopped
6 eggs	2 tablespoons cinnamon
2 egg yolks	½ cup chocolate morsels
3 cups heavy cream	10 ounces chocolate morsels
½ cup bourbon	8 ounces heavy cream
1 loaf challah bread	1 teaspoon vanilla extract
1 cup light brown sugar	Powdered sugar, for garnish
1 ½ cups sugar	

Preparation:

1. For bread pudding: start by preheating the oven to 350°F. In a mixing bowl, whisk together the vanilla, eggs, yolks, heavy cream, and bourbon. Set aside.

2. Separate the challah bread into sections of 6. Slice each section, first by slicing in half horizontally and then quartering. Place the cut challah bread into a large mixing bowl. Pour both of the sugars, pecans, cinnamon, and chocolate morsels onto the cut challah bread. Mix together. Pour the cream mixture over the rolls and gently stir to evenly coat the bread mixture.

3. Spray a 9" x 13" baking dish with nonstick food spray. Pour the bread mixture into the baking dish and smooth out the top with a spatula. Spray a piece of aluminum foil with nonstick food spray and cover the baking dish. Bake for 90 minutes covered, then remove the foil and bake for an additional 30 minutes. Remove from the oven when an inserted toothpick comes out clean. Let cool.

4. For sauce: place the chocolate, heavy cream and vanilla in a double boiler. Heat through until the chocolate is melted, stir until the sauce forms, and then remove from the heat and keep warm.

5. To finish the dessert, cut the bread pudding into squares or use a biscuit cutter to section off into round portions.

Serving Suggestion: Serve warm with a few spoonful's of the chocolate sauce and garnish with powdered sugar, if desired.

Variation Tip: Use whipped cream also.

Nutritional Information per Serving:

Calories 377|Carbohydrates 72g|Protein 7.7g|Fat 7.3g|Sodium 190mg|Fiber 1.4g

Death by Butter Beer Cupcakes

Prep Time: 15 minutes|Cook Time: 25 minutes|Servings: 18 cupcakes

Ingredients

Cupcakes

2 cups all-purpose flour	1 teaspoon butter extract
1 teaspoon baking powder	seeds from one vanilla bean,
1 teaspoon baking soda	divided
½ teaspoon salt	½ cup buttermilk
1 cup brown sugar	½ cup pumpkin beer
3 large eggs	1 cup toffee bits, optional
½ cup canola oil	

Butter beer Sauce

1 (11-ounce) bag butterscotch chips	2 teaspoons unsulfured molasses
½ cup heavy cream	1¾ cups powdered sugar or more, if desired
1 tablespoon honey	
treacle butter frosting + chocolate pretzels	3 tablespoons unsweetened cocoa powder
30 to 40 mini pretzel twists	1 teaspoon vanilla extract
9 ounces semi-sweet or milk chocolate, melted	1 teaspoon butter extract
	⅓ cup butter beer sauce
8 tablespoons salted butter, softened	2 tablespoons heavy whipping cream

Preparation

1. Preheat the oven to 350°F. Line 2 standard cupcake trays with 18 liners.

2. In a medium-sized mixing bowl, combine the flour, baking powder, baking soda, salt and brown sugar.

3. In another bowl, combine the eggs, canola oil, butter extract, seeds from half a vanilla bean and the buttermilk. Beat until smooth.

4. Slowly add the dry

5. Ingredients to the wet

6. Ingredients with the mixer on low until there are no longer any clumps of flour.

7. Add the beer and mix until combined. The batter should be pourable, but not super thin.

8. Fill the liners ¾ full. Bake for about 18 to 22 minutes. Allow to cool completely before frosting.

9. For the butter beer sauce: Add the butterscotch chips, cream and honey to a small pot. Set over low heat, stirring often until melted and smooth. Remove from heat.

10. For the frosting: Melt chocolate in the microwave in 30 second intervals, stirring between each, until smooth. Dip each pretzel in chocolate, allowing the excess to drip off. Place on wax paper lined cookie sheets and chill in the freezer until firm, about 10 minutes.

11. Add the butter, molasses and powdered sugar to a bowl and beat together until the butter is light and fluffy, about 4 minutes.

12. Add the cocoa powder, vanilla and butter extract. Beat until there are no streaks of white. Beat in ⅓ cup of butter beer sauce and the seeds from ½ of the remaining vanilla bean until smooth and creamy.

13. Add 2 tablespoons of the heavy cream and whip the frosting for 2 to 4 minutes or until light and fluffy. Taste the frosting and add more powdered sugar if you like a sweeter or thicker frosting.

14. Take about ⅓ to ½ of the chocolate-covered pretzels and finely chop them. Stir the pretzels into the frosting. Skip this step if you like a smooth frosting.

15. To assemble the cupcakes: Pipe frosting onto each cupcake. Garnish each cupcake with a chocolate covered pretzel.

Serving Suggestion: Drizzle each cupcake with butterbeer sauce just before serving.

Variation Tip: Stir toffee bits into the cupcake mix for a crunch.

Nutritional Information Per Serving:
Calories 120|Carbohydrates 19.3g|Protein 1.09g|Fat 4.64g|Sodium 136mg|Fiber 0.3g

Giant Blueberry Muffins with Crumb Topping

Prep Time: 20 minutes|Cook Time: 30 minutes|Servings: 18

Ingredients:

Crumb Topping:
1 cup all-purpose flour
3 tablespoons light brown sugar
2 tablespoons granulated sugar

1 teaspoon baking powder
Pinch of salt
6 tablespoons unsalted butter, melted

Muffins:
1 ¾ cups all-purpose flour
2 ¼ teaspoon baking powder
½ teaspoon salt
1 cup granulated sugar
2 large eggs

½ cup canola oil
¾ cup whole milk
1 teaspoon pure vanilla extract
1 ½ cups blueberries

Preparation:

1. Preheat the oven to 375°F. Line 18 muffin cups with paper or foil liners or spray 2 muffin tins with cooking spray.
2. In a medium bowl, combine the flour with the brown sugar, granulated sugar, baking powder and salt. Stir in the melted butter, and then pinch the mixture until it forms pea-size clumps.
3. In a medium bowl, whisk the flour with the baking powder and salt. In a large bowl, combine the sugar, eggs and canola oil and beat with a handheld electric mixer at low speed until combined. Beat in the whole milk and vanilla. Add the flour mixture all at once and beat at low speed until the batter is smooth. Stir in the blueberries.
4. Spoon the batter into 18 of the cups, filling them about three-quarters full. Sprinkle the crumb topping on top of each one and bake for about 30 minutes or until the muffins are golden and a toothpick inserted in the center comes out with a few moist crumbs attached. Let the blueberry muffins cool in the pan for 10 minutes before serving.

Serving Suggestion: Serve warm with chocolate tea.
Variation Tip: Drizzle blueberry sauce for extra flavoring.

Nutritional Information per Serving:
Calories 211.3|Carbohydrates 30.8g|Protein 3.1g|Fat 8.6g|Sodium 199.6mg|Fiber 1g

Sponge Cake

Prep Time: 10 minutes|Cook Time: 30 minutes|Servings: 1

Ingredients

1 cup flour
1 teaspoon baking powder
8 tablespoons butter, room temperature
½ cup sugar

1 egg + 1 egg white, room temperature
¼ cup raspberry jam
¼ cup strawberry jam
whipped cream, for serving

Preparation

1. Preheat the oven to 350°F and line two ramekins.
2. In a small bowl, mix together the flour and baking powder.
3. Use a stand mixer to cream together the sugar, butter, and eggs. Slowly pour in the dry ingredient mix and stir on medium until a smooth batter forms.
4. Pour about ½ cup of the batter into each ramekin. Cook for 20 to 25 minutes or until the tops of the cakes are golden brown and a toothpick inserted in the center comes out clean. Remove from the oven.
5. Let the cakes rest in their ramekins for about 10 minutes before taking them out and leave them to cool down completely.
6. Spread strawberry and raspberry jam onto each layer and press the cakes together to form a sandwich.
7. Spread the whipped cream evenly on the cake sandwich and serve.

Serving Suggestion: None.
Variation Tip: Add chocolate ganache.
Nutritional Information Per Serving:
Calories 187|Carbohydrates 36g|Protein 5g|Fat 2.7g|Sodium 144mg|Fiber 1g

Rhubarb Crumble

Prep Time: 45 minutes|Cook Time: 30 minutes|Servings: 12

Ingredients:

8 cups chopped fresh or frozen rhubarb
1 ¼ cups sugar, divided
2 ½ cups all-purpose flour

¼ cup packed brown sugar
¼ cup quick-cooking oats
1 cup cold butter

Custard sauce:
6 large egg yolks
½ cup sugar

2 cups heavy whipping cream
1 ¼ teaspoons vanilla extract

Preparation:

1. In a saucepan, combine rhubarb and ¾ cup sugar. Cover and cook over medium heat, stirring occasionally, until the rhubarb is tender, about 10 minutes.
2. Pour into a greased 13x9-in. baking dish. In a bowl, combine flour, brown sugar, oats and remaining sugar. Cut in butter until crumbly; sprinkle over rhubarb. Bake at 400°F for 30 minutes.
3. Meanwhile, in a saucepan, whisk the egg yolks and sugar; stir in cream. Cook and stir over low heat until a thermometer reads 160°F and mixture thickens, 15-20 minutes. Remove from the heat; stir in vanilla.

Serving Suggestion: Serve warm over rhubarb crumble.
Variation Tip: Add dill and chives for freshness. ·
Nutritional Information per Serving:
Calories 550|Carbohydrates 60g|Protein 6g|Fat 33g|Sodium 179mg|Fiber 2g

Fruitcake

Prep Time: 30 minutes|Cook Time: 2 hours|Servings: 18

Ingredients:

2 ¼ cups all-purpose flour
½ cup finely ground almonds
1 teaspoon ground cinnamon
½ teaspoon ground allspice
¼ teaspoon ground nutmeg
⅛ teaspoon ground cloves
¼ teaspoon salt
2 stick unsalted butter, at room temperature
1 ¼ cups packed dark brown sugar

Grated zest of 1 orange
Grated zest of 1 lemon
4 large eggs, at room temperature
½ cup orange marmalade
½ cup dark raisins
½ cup golden raisins
½ cup dried currants or sweetened dried cranberries
¼ cup apple juice (or brandy)

Preparation:

1. Preheat the oven to 350°F. Grease and flour a 9" round cake pan that is at least 2 inches deep.
2. In a large mixing bowl, whisk together the flour, ground almonds, spices, and salt.
3. In another large bowl, cream together the butter, sugar, and zest of the orange and lemon with an electric mixer, scraping down the sides as needed, until light and fluffy, about 5 minutes.
4. Add the eggs, one at a time, beating well after each until incorporated.
5. Beat in the marmalade.
6. Stir in the flour mixture, then the raisins and cranberries, then stir in the apple juice.
7. With a spatula, give one final stir to be sure the batter is evenly mixed.
8. Scrape the batter into the prepared pan and bake for 2 hours.
9. Remove the cake from the oven and leave it in the pan to cool for a while.
10. Flip the cake out onto a serving platter. It should either be eaten then day it is made or wrapped really well in plastic wrap and freeze it for up to 2 months.

Serving Suggestion: Serve warm with cold milk.
Variation Tip: Add your favorite dry fruits for crunch.
Nutritional Information per Serving:
Calories 360|Carbohydrates 59.9g|Protein 4.3g|Fat 4.3g|Sodium 267mg|Fiber 0g

Molly's Chocolate Mocha Sourdough Bundt Cake

Prep Time: 20 minutes|Cook Time: 45 minutes|Servings: 12

Ingredients:

1 ¼ cup sugar
½ cup unsalted butter, room temperature
1 cup sourdough starter (discard or active)
2 cups all-purpose flour

1 cup brewed coffee, room temperature
3 eggs
2 teaspoons vanilla extract
3 tablespoons baker's cocoa
3 tablespoons vegetable oil

1 teaspoon baking powder
1 teaspoon baking soda
Chocolate Ganache:
4 ounces bittersweet chocolate, finely chopped
1 ½ tablespoon corn syrup

½ teaspoon salt

½ cup heavy cream
1 ½ tablespoon brown sugar
1 pinch salt

Preparation:

1. Preheat the oven to 350°F and prepare the Bundt pan with butter and flour.
2. In a large mixing bowl, combine the butter and sugar with a fork until combined.
3. Add the eggs, one at a time, and whisk until combined.
4. Whisk in the vanilla extract. Add the flour, brewed coffee, cocoa powder, vegetable oil, baking powder, baking soda, and sourdough starter to the bowl. Whisk until combined.
5. Pour into the prepared Bundt pan.
6.6 Bake for 35 minutes, or until a toothpick inserted inside comes out clean.
7. Cool in the pan for 10 minutes, and then turn out onto a cooling rack.
8. Chocolate Ganache: Place the chopped chocolate, the corn syrup, and a pinch of salt in a medium bowl.
9. Place the heavy cream and the sugar into a small saucepan and heat on a skillet until just hot enough to melt the sugar. Make sure you stir occasionally.
10. Pour the hot milk and sugar mixture over the chocolate.
11. Whisk until it is smooth. Drizzle over the cooled cake.

Serving Suggestion: Serve slices with chilled beer.
Variation Tip: Add nuts in the ganache.
Nutritional Information per Serving:
Calories 423|Carbohydrates 52g|Protein 7g|Fat 21g|Sodium 272mg|Fiber 3g

Egg-cellent Eggy Bread

Prep Time: 5 minutes|Cook Time: 6 minutes|Servings: 2

Ingredients:
1 teaspoon curry powder
¼ cup milk
4 slices whole grain bread
4 eggs
1 handful chives, finely chopped
2 scallions, finely chopped
2 teaspoons olive oil
Salt and pepper, to taste

Preparation:
1. Beat the eggs in a bowl and add the chopped scallions and chives.
2. Stir in the milk, curry powder, salt, and pepper.
3. Take each slice of bread and soak it in the mixture.
4. Add the olive oil to a skillet and warm it up. Fry the bread slices for a minute on each side until crispy.
5. Serve and enjoy!

Serving Suggestions: Serve with maple syrup on top.
Variation Tip: You can also add chopped tomatoes to the mixture.
Nutritional Information per Serving:
Calories: 552|Fat: 28.42g|Sat Fat: 7.091g|Carbohydrates: 42.94g|Fiber: 7.4g|Sugar: 10.07g|Protein: 30.62g

Golden Snitch Truffles

Prep Time: 15 minutes|Cook Time: 0 minutes|Servings: 12

Ingredients:
18 chocolate sandwich cookies
4 ounces cream cheese
Gold sprinkles

Preparation:
1. Finely blend the sandwich cookies in a food processor.
2. Put the crushed cookies and cream cheese in a bowl, and mix well to form a dough.
3. Make balls from the dough using a tablespoon for each.
4. Fill a small bowl with the sprinkles and roll the balls in the sprinkles to coat them.
5. Refrigerate for at least 30 minutes.
6. Serve and enjoy!

Serving Suggestions: Serve with orange juice.
Variation Tip: Add toothpicks to each ball before serving.
Nutritional Information per Serving:
Calories: 111|Fat: 6.15g|Sat Fat: 2.72g|Carbohydrates: 13.12g|Fiber: 0.5g|Sugar: 7.66g|Protein: 1.61g

Butterbeer Pancakes

Prep Time: 10 minutes|Cook Time: 10 minutes|Servings: 4

Ingredients:

For the pancakes:

1 large egg

¼ cup caramel coffee creamer

¼ cup ricotta cheese

¼ teaspoon salt

½ cup whole milk

¼ teaspoon baking soda

½ teaspoon baking powder

2 tablespoons granulated sugar

1½ cups flour

½ cup butterscotch chips

For the syrup:

⅛ cup butter

4 tablespoons buttermilk

½ teaspoon butter extract

¼ teaspoon baking soda

¼ cup sugar

Preparation:

1. Put the butterscotch chips in a food processor and pulse them into a crumb texture. Place them in a large bowl.
2. Add the flour, sugar, baking powder, soda, and salt to the butterscotch crumbs and mix well.
3. Whisk together the milk, ricotta, coffee creamer, and eggs in another bowl.
4. Add the wet mixture to the flour mixture and stir until the batter is well combined.
5. Coat a large pan over medium heat with cooking oil and heat it up. Add the batter a ¼ cup at a time for each pancake.
6. Cook each side of the pancakes for about 1–2 minutes until golden brown.
7. For the syrup, take a saucepan and add the butter, buttermilk, and sugar.
8. Stir on medium heat until the sugar dissolves.
9. Now, stir in the baking soda and butter extract. Let the mixture sit for a few minutes.
10. Serve the pancakes with the syrup drizzled on top.
11. Enjoy!

Serving Suggestions: Serve with whipped cream on top.
Variation Tip: You can also use vanilla extract.
Nutritional Information per Serving:
Calories: 811|Fat: 57.37g|Sat Fat: 36.964g|Carbohydrates: 65.88g|Fiber: 1.3g|Sugar: 29.16g|Protein: 9.56g

English Fried Eggs with Gammon

Prep Time: 5 minutes|Cook Time: 4 minutes|Servings: 1

Ingredients:

2 large eggs

2 slices gammon

Salt and ground black pepper, to taste

Preparation:

1. In a skillet, fry the gammon in a little oil over medium heat. Cook for 2 minutes on each side.
2. Remove the gammon and let it drain on a paper towel.
3. Break the eggs into the same skillet and season with salt and pepper.
4. Fry the eggs in the gammon fat until they begin to sizzle and are cooked to your liking.
5. Place the fried eggs on top of the gammon slices.
6. Enjoy!

Serving Suggestions: Serve with oregano on top.
Variation Tip: You can add some cayenne pepper.
Nutritional Information per Serving:
Calories: 600|Fat: 28.2g|Sat Fat: 9.747g|Carbohydrates: 11.98g|Fiber: 0.7g|Sugar: 8.99g|Protein: 76.68g

Charming Curry Puffs

Nutritional Information per Serving:
Calories: 468|Fat: 17.31g|Sat Fat: 5.823g|Carbohydrates: 51.02g|Fiber: 10.7g|Sugar: 4.22g|Protein: 28.76g

Fantastic Fried Sausage Patties

Prep Time: 15 minutes|Cook Time: 30 minutes|Servings: 3

Ingredients:

2 sheets puff pastry	into ½-inch cubes
½ pound ground beef	2 green onions, chopped
4 tablespoons curry powder	Salt, to taste
2 potatoes, peeled and diced	1 egg, beaten

Preparation:

1. Put the ground beef, green onions, curry powder, salt, and potatoes in a saucepan with a little oil over medium heat.
2. Cook until the beef and potatoes are thoroughly cooked. (You can add a little water to help the potatoes cook.)
3. Remove from the heat, drain any fat, and let the mixture cool (about 30 minutes).
4. Preheat the oven to 400°F. Line two baking sheets with parchment paper.
5. Cut each pastry sheet into four equal squares and place them on the baking sheets.
6. Place a tablespoonful of the beef mixture into the center of each pastry square, then brush the edges with a little of the beaten egg.
7. Fold each square over the filling to make a triangle and press to close completely using a fork. Brush the tops with the rest of the egg.
8. Bake for about 20 minutes or until golden brown.
9. Serve and enjoy!

Serving Suggestions: Serve with ketchup.
Variation Tip: You can use ground chicken instead of beef.

Prep Time: 5 minutes|Cook Time: 10 minutes|Servings: 6

Ingredients:

½ pound ground veal	⅛ teaspoon dried marjoram
½ pound ground pork or beef	⅛ teaspoon ground thyme
1 cup fresh breadcrumbs	¼ teaspoon freshly ground
1 teaspoon lemon zest, grated	black pepper
1 teaspoon salt	2 egg yolks
¼ teaspoon ground nutmeg	2 tablespoons butter
1 teaspoon ground sage	

Preparation:

1. Combine all the ingredients except the butter in a large bowl.
2. Put the butter in a large skillet over medium heat.
3. Form the meat into sausage shapes and fry them for around 5 minutes on each side or until brown.
4. Transfer the sausages to a paper towel-lined plate.
5. Serve and enjoy!

Serving Suggestions: Serve with mashed potatoes.
Variation Tip: You can use margarine or oil instead of butter.
Nutritional Information per Serving:
Calories: 330|Fat: 26.98g|Sat Fat: 10.6g|Carbohydrates: 3.28g|Fiber: 0.2g|Sugar: 0.39g|Protein: 17.17g

Scottish Porridge

Prep Time: 5 minutes|Cook Time: 12 minutes|Servings: 4

Ingredients:

1 cup Scottish oats

1½ cups milk

1½ cups water

½ teaspoon ground nutmeg

½ teaspoon ground cinnamon

¼ teaspoon sea salt

Preparation:

1. Add the oats, milk, water, and salt to a saucepan over medium heat and cook for 5–7 minutes, stirring occasionally.

2. Stir in the nutmeg and cinnamon.

3. Cook for another 1–2 minutes until the mixture becomes thick.

4. Remove from the heat and let it cool.

5. Serve and enjoy!

Serving Suggestions: Serve with a topping of chopped strawberries or raspberries.

Variation Tip: You can also add vanilla extract.

Nutritional Information per Serving:

Calories: 116|Fat: 4.75g|Sat Fat: 2.091g|Carbohydrates: 20.33g|Fiber: 3.8g|Sugar: 4.98g|Protein: 6.98g

Sorcerer's Salad

Prep Time: 20 minutes|Cook Time: 20 minutes|Servings: 4

Ingredients:

1 cucumber, spiralized

1 cup prepared seaweed salad

16 ounces calamari rings and tentacles

3 tablespoons black sesame

seeds

1 tablespoon rice vinegar

3 tablespoons mayonnaise

1 tablespoon sesame oil

Salt and pepper, to taste

Preparation:

1. Heat the sesame oil in a skillet over medium heat.

2. Add the calamari rings and tentacles to the pan.

3. Season with salt and pepper and cook for 1–2 minutes, until tender.

4. Remove from the heat and let the calamari cool.

5. Take a small bowl, and whisk together the mayonnaise, rice vinegar, and black sesame seeds.

6. Put the cucumber spirals and seaweed salad in a large bowl.

7. Pour the dressing on top and toss gently to coat evenly.

8. Place the calamari on top of the salad.

9. Serve and enjoy!

Serving Suggestions: Serve with the black sesame seeds sprinkled on top.

Variation Tip: You can use olive oil instead.

Nutritional Information per Serving:

Calories: 434|Fat: 26.99g|Sat Fat: 3.791g|Carbohydrates: 42.95g|Fiber: 4g|Sugar: 7.47g|Protein: 7.16g

Captivating Cinnamon Rolls

Prep Time: 40 minutes|Cook Time: 20 minutes|Servings: 6

Ingredients:

½ cup milk, warmed
1 tablespoon sweetener
½ tablespoon active dry yeast
1¼ cups flour
1 tablespoon baking powder
½ cup sugar
¼ teaspoon salt
1 tablespoon cinnamon
2 tablespoons oil
1 teaspoon pure vanilla extract

Preparation:

1. Put the warmed milk in a bowl.
2. Stir in the sweetener and sprinkle with the yeast. Set aside for 5 minutes.
3. Put the flour, baking powder, sugar, salt, and cinnamon in another bowl and stir to combine.
4. Stir the oil and vanilla extract into the milk mixture.
5. Add the milk mixture to the flour mixture and combine to form a dough.
6. Place the dough in a greased bowl, cover it loosely, and leave it in a warm place for about 30 minutes.
7. Once the dough has doubled in size, put some flour on a clean kitchen surface and roll the dough out evenly into a very thin rectangle (just under ¼-inch thick).
8. Give the flour-milk mixture another stir and spread it evenly over the dough.
9. Cut long strips of the covered dough and roll each up as tightly as possible.
10. Place the rolls in a greased baking pan and loosely cover them for 30 minutes.
11. Preheat the oven to 325°F and bake the rolls for about 20 minutes.
12. Serve hot and enjoy!

Serving Suggestions: Serve with cream cheese frosting on top.
Variation Tip: You can use whole wheat pastry flour instead.
Nutritional Information per Serving:
Calories: 198|Fat: 5.57g|Sat Fat: 1.145g|Carbohydrates: 33.64g|Fiber: 1.7g|Sugar: 10.93g|Protein: 3.79g

Down East Maine Pumpkin Bread

Prep Time: 15 minutes|Cook Time: 50 minutes|Servings: 24

Ingredients:

1 (15 ounces) can pumpkin puree
4 eggs
1 cup vegetable oil
⅔ cup water
3 cups white sugar
3½ cups all-purpose flour
2 teaspoons baking soda
1½ teaspoons salt
1 teaspoon ground cinnamon
1 teaspoon ground nutmeg
½ teaspoon ground cloves
¼ teaspoon ground ginger

Preparation:

1. Preheat oven to 350°F. Grease and flour three 7x3 inch loaf pans.
2. In a large bowl, mix together pumpkin puree, eggs, oil, water and sugar until well blended.
3. In a separate bowl, whisk together the flour, baking soda, salt, cinnamon, nutmeg, cloves and ginger. Stir the dry ingredients into the pumpkin mixture until just blended. Pour into the prepared pans.
4. Bake for about 50 minutes in the preheated oven. Loaves are done when toothpick inserted in center comes out clean.

Serving Suggestion: Serve cold topped with butter and along with tea.
Variation Tip: Use nuts for crunch.
Nutritional Information per Serving:
Calories 263|Carbohydrates 40.6g|Protein 3.1g|Fat 10.3g|Sodium 305.4mg|Fiber 2g

Potent Pesto Toast

Prep Time: 5 minutes|Cook Time: 6 minutes|Servings: 2

Ingredients:

1-pound large shrimp, peeled and deveined
1 tablespoon olive oil
½ cup cherry tomatoes, cut in half
Salt and black pepper, to taste
¼ cup pesto
4 large slices whole wheat bread, lightly toasted
¼ cup roasted red bell peppers, thinly sliced
1 cup arugula

Preparation:

1. Heat the olive oil in a large skillet over medium heat. Add the shrimp and the tomatoes with salt and pepper.
2. Cook for 4 minutes, stirring often, until the shrimp are nearly cooked through.
3. Reduce the heat, stir in the pesto, and cook until the shrimp are completely done for another minute or so.
4. Add the shrimp and tomatoes to the toasted bread, followed by the peppers and arugula.
5. Top with the sauce from the skillet.
6. Serve and enjoy!

Serving Suggestions: Serve topped with crumbled feta cheese.
Variation Tip: You can use any type of thick bread you prefer.
Nutritional Information per Serving:
Calories: 420|Fat: 26.34g|Sat Fat: 4.318g|Carbohydrates: 34.65g|Fiber: 7.1g|Sugar: 8.34g|Protein: 13.33g

Bacon Cheddar Ale Bread

Prep Time: 10 minutes|Cook Time: 55 minutes|Servings: 1 loaf

Ingredients

3 cups self-rising flour
3 tablespoons sugar
12 ounces ale
1 cup cooked bacon, chopped
1 cup cheddar, shredded
1 tablespoon dried thyme
¼ cup melted butter
cooking spray

Preparation

1. Preheat oven to 375°F and grease your loaf pan.
2. Combine flour, sugar and ale in a bowl. Mix together till well combined. This will look like dough like batter. Fold in thyme, bacon, and cheese.
3. Pour the doughy mixture into your greased loaf pan. Smooth top and make sure the dough fills the pan.
4. Bake for 45 minutes.
5. Remove from the oven and pour the melted butter over top of your loaf.
6. Bake for 10 more minutes. (Your butter may still look bubbly when done, this is ok)
7. Remove from oven. Allow the loaf to cool.
8. Remove from loaf pan and serve.

Serving Suggestion: Serve cold topped with peanut butter.
Variation Tip: Use diced carrots instead of bacon.
Nutritional Information Per Serving:
Calories 160|Carbohydrates 23g|Protein 7g|Fat 4g|Sodium 270mg|Fiber 2g

Cinnamon Pull-Apart Breakfast Rolls

Prep Time: 40 minutes|Cook Time: 20 minutes|Servings: 12

Ingredients:

Dough:

¼ cup water warm
1 tablespoon yeast active dry
1 tablespoon sugar
⅔ cups milk whole
½ stick butter

3 cups all-purpose flour
½ teaspoon salt
2 large egg
⅓ cup sugar

Cinnamon Filling:

1 tablespoon butter melted
¼ cup brown sugar dark,

packed
1 tablespoon cinnamon

Icing:

1 cup powdered sugar sifted
4 ounces cream cheese softened

½ teaspoon vanilla extract
1 tablespoon heavy cream

Preparation:

1. Dough: Combine water, yeast, and first sugar in a mixing bowl and set aside until puffy.
2. Heat milk and butter in a small saucepan or the microwave until the butter is melted. Set aside.
3. In a separate bowl, whisk together eggs and second sugar. Then whisk in the milk-butter mixture. Whisk together flour and salt. Set aside.
4. Add yeast mixture and egg mixture to flour mixture and mix together. Knead dough in mixing bowl of an electric mixer with dough hook until dough is smooth and elastic, about 10 minutes.
5. Place dough in an oiled bowl, turning to coat, and cover with plastic wrap. Set aside in a warm place until doubled in size, 1 ½–2 hours.
6. Cinnamon Filling: Combine the brown sugar and cinnamon. Set aside. Grease and flour a 9" x 13" pan.
7. Turn the dough out onto a lightly floured surface and roll into a 16" x 12" rectangle. Brush the tablespoon of melted butter over the dough. Spread filling over the dough, leaving a ½" gap on all sides. Roll up the long side. Slice off the messy ends.
8. A clean Preparation to cut the roll is using dental floss. First, slide a length of floss under the roll until you reach the center.
9. Bring the two ends over the roll and cross them, pulling until a neat cut has been made. Cut the log into 12 equal pieces.
10. Lay the rolls in the greased pan. Allow to rise until rolls are just touching each other, 1 ½–2 hours.
11. Adjust the oven rack to the middle position and preheat the oven to 350°F.
Bake the rolls for 20 minutes until golden brown, rotating the pan halfway through baking.
12. Remove from the oven. Cool for 10 minutes in the pan. Invert the pan and re-invert the rolls onto a serving platter.
13. Icing: Beat the icing ingredients together until smooth. Sifting the sugar will make this easier.

Serving Suggestion: Spread icing over the rolls while they are still warm & serve immediately.
Variation Tip: Drizzle chocolate ganache.
Nutritional Information per Serving:
Calories 249|Carbohydrates 40.9g|Protein 5.4g|Fat 7.3g|Sodium 607.5mg|Fiber 0.1g

Dinner Recipes

Apprentice's Roast Beef

Prep Time: 10 minutes|Cook Time: 1 hour 30 minutes|Servings: 2

Ingredients:
3 pounds boneless rump roast
1 tablespoon olive oil
3 teaspoons salt
1 teaspoon pepper
3 cloves garlic, sliced

Preparation:
1. Rub salt over the roast evenly.
2. Preheat the oven to 375°F.
3. Make small slits in the roast and put the sliced garlic in each slit.
4. Now, rub the meat with olive oil and sprinkle with pepper.
5. Place the roast in a baking pan in the preheated oven.
6. Bake for about 30 minutes.
7. After 30 minutes, lower the temperature to 225°F, then bake for another hour.
8. When done, remove the roast and let it cool for some time.
9. Cut into thin slices.
10. Serve and enjoy!

Serving Suggestions: Serve with melted butter on top.
Variation Tip: Fresh rosemary can also be used.
Nutritional Information per Serving:
Calories: 1565|Fat: 84.25g|Sat Fat: 28.694g|Carbohydrates: 3.62g|Fiber: 0.4g|Sugar: 1.19g|Protein: 199.41g

Bewitching Braised Lamb Chops

Prep Time: 10 minutes|Cook Time: 25 minutes|Servings: 4

Ingredients:
4 lamb chops
3 tablespoons vegetable oil
Salt and ground black pepper, to taste
1 medium onion, chopped
1 tablespoon flour
1 cup white wine
1 teaspoon dried rosemary leaves
½ teaspoon ground sage

Preparation:
1. Add a tablespoon of oil to a skillet over medium heat.
2. Season the lamb chops with salt and pepper on both sides.
3. Place the lamb chops on the skillet and cook for about 3 minutes, turning now and then.
4. Remove the chops from the skillet and set them aside.
5. Put the onion with the remaining oil in the skillet and cook until just brown.
6. Sprinkle in the flour and stir well.
7. Pour in the wine while stirring.
8. Stir in the rosemary and sage.
9. Place the lamb chops back in the skillet and cook for another 15–20 minutes.
10. Serve and enjoy!

Serving Suggestions: Serve with mashed potatoes.
Variation Tip: You can add some fresh mint.
Nutritional Information per Serving:
Calories: 759|Fat: 41.54g|Sat Fat: 20.89g|Carbohydrates: 6.01g|Fiber: 0.9g|Sugar: 2.38g|Protein: 91.67g

Headmaster's Yule Ball Pork Chops

9. Serve warm and enjoy!

Serving Suggestions: Serve with the apple and onion over the pork.
Variation Tip: Check if the pork chops are properly cooked before removing them from the pan.
Nutritional Information per Serving:
Calories: 364|Fat: 13.39g|Sat Fat: 3.243g|Carbohydrates: 17.79g|Fiber: 2.6g|Sugar: 12.84g|Protein: 41.96g

Wizard's Bacon and Cheddar Ale Bread

Prep Time: 5 minutes|Cook Time: 10 minutes|Servings: 4

Ingredients:

4 boneless pork chops
1 teaspoon flour
1 teaspoon salt
1½ teaspoons rubbed sage
1 teaspoon garlic, minced
1 teaspoon thyme leaves
½ teaspoon all-spice

½ teaspoon paprika
2 tablespoons olive oil
1 onion, thinly sliced
2 apples, thinly sliced
½ cup apple juice
1 tablespoon brown sugar

Preparation:
1. Mix the flour, salt, sage, garlic, thyme, all-spice, and paprika in a small bowl.
2. Sprinkle half the seasoning mixture on both sides of the pork chops evenly.
3. Put a skillet over medium heat and warm the oil.
4. Place the pork chops in the skillet and cook both sides until brown.
5. Remove the pork chops, add the sliced onion and cook for about 3 minutes.
6. Add the sliced apples into the pan and cook for another 2 minutes.
7. Add the apple juice, brown sugar, and remaining seasoning mixture to another bowl.
8. Place the pork chops back in the skillet and pour the juice mixture into the pan. Bring it to the boil.

Prep Time: 10 minutes|Cook Time: 55 minutes|Servings: 1

Ingredients:

1 cup cheddar cheese, shredded
1 tablespoon dried thyme
12 ounces medium-bodied pale ale

1 cup bacon, cooked and chopped
¼ cup butter, melted
3 cups self-rising flour
3 tablespoon sugar

Preparation:
1. Preheat the oven to 375°F. Grease a baking pan with cooking spray.
2. Put the flour, sugar, and ale in a large bowl. Mix well.
3. Stir in the thyme, bacon, and cheese, then pour the mixture into the greased pan.
4. Place the pan in the preheated oven and bake for 45 minutes.
5. Remove from the oven and pour the melted butter on top.
6. Bake for another 10 minutes.
7. Remove from the oven and set aside to let it cool.
8. Serve and enjoy!

Serving Suggestions: Serve with hot sauce.
Variation Tip: You can also add cayenne pepper.
Nutritional Information per Serving:
Calories: 2394|Fat: 92.35g|Sat Fat: 36.478g|Carbohydrates: 341.93g|Fiber: 14.2g|Sugar: 54g|Protein: 53.22g

Elves' French Onion Soup

Prep Time: 10 minutes|Cook Time: 40 minutes|Servings: 4

Ingredients:

4 medium onions, thinly sliced
½ cup butter, melted
1 baguette, sliced into 1-inch thick pieces
½ cup parmesan cheese, grated

1 teaspoon salt
¼ teaspoon ground black pepper
¼ teaspoon sugar
1 tablespoon flour
6 cups beef stock

Preparation:

1. Preheat the oven to 350°F.
2. Put the pieces of bread on a cookie sheet.
3. Put the melted butter in a small dish. Dip a pastry brush into the butter from the pot and brush each side of the pieces of bread.
4. Sprinkle the cheese on top.
5. Place the bread in the oven and toast for about 10 minutes until brown.
6. Add the remaining butter to a skillet and heat it over medium heat.
7. Add the onions, salt, and pepper, then stir in the sugar.
8. Cook for about 15 minutes until the onions brown.
9. Blend in the flour and bring the soup to a boil.
10. Serve warm and enjoy!

Serving Suggestions: Serve with the toasted cheesy bread pieces on top.
Variation Tip: You can also add cayenne pepper.
Nutritional Information per Serving:
Calories: 316|Fat: 26.92g|Sat Fat: 16.65g|Carbohydrates: 8.82g|Fiber: 0.2g|Sugar: 2.65g|Protein: 11.28g

Sunday Roast Chicken

Prep Time: 15 minutes|Cook Time: 1 hour 40 minutes|Servings: 4

Ingredients:

3 pounds whole chicken
2 garlic cloves
1 large onion, cut into wedges
1 lemon, cut in half
4 tablespoons unsalted butter, softened

1 tablespoon Italian parsley, chopped
1 tablespoon fresh thyme, chopped
2 bay leaves
Salt and ground black pepper

Preparation:

1. Preheat the oven to 400°F.
2. Mix the butter, parsley, thyme, salt, and pepper in a bowl.
3. Rub the butter mixture over the chicken evenly.
4. Place the chicken on a baking pan with the onion wedges, lemon halves, bay leaves, and garlic.
5. Place the pan in the preheated oven and roast for about 1 hour and 40 minutes.
6. Remove the chicken from the oven and allow it to rest slightly before serving.
7. Enjoy!

Serving Suggestions: Serve with roasted potatoes.
Variation Tip: Make gravy from the pan juices.
Nutritional Information per Serving:
Calories: 600|Fat: 20.12g|Sat Fat: 7.88g|Carbohydrates: 6.47g|Fiber: 1.1g|Sugar: 2.49g|Protein: 93.55g

Philosopher's Roast Potatoes

Prep Time: 10 minutes|Cook Time: 45 minutes|Servings: 2

Ingredients:

6 red potatoes, scrubbed and chopped
¼ cup olive oil
1 teaspoon salt
1 teaspoon rosemary, dried
2 cloves garlic, minced
Ground black pepper, to taste

Preparation:

1. Preheat the oven to 400°F.
2. In a bowl, sprinkle the potatoes with salt, oil, rosemary, garlic, and black pepper.
3. Spread the coated potatoes in a roasting pan and place them in the preheated oven.
4. Bake the potatoes for about 45 minutes, until crispy and golden.
5. Serve and enjoy!

Serving Suggestions: Serve with your choice of meat.
Variation Tip: You can adjust the amount of herbs according to your taste.
Nutritional Information per Serving:
Calories: 102|Fat: 4g|Sat Fat: 0.5g|Carbohydrates: 18g|Fiber: 1.9g|Sugar: 1.4g|Protein: 2g

Barbosa Cake Recipe

Prep Time: 15 minutes|Cook Time: 25 minutes|Servings: 12

Ingredients:
Semolina Cake:

2 cups semolina flour
1 cup plain yogurt
½ cup granulated sugar
½ cup ghee, melted
½ cup unsweetened coconut
flakes
2 teaspoons baking powder
2 teaspoons vanilla extract
1 teaspoon salt

Simple Syrup:

1 ¼ cup sugar
1 ¼ cup water
2 teaspoons vanilla extract

Toppings:
⅓ cup chopped mix nuts

Preparation:

1. Preheat the oven to 350°F. Line a 10" cake plate with a parchment paper circle cut to size and brush all the edges with a little melted ghee.
2. In a large bowl, mix the ingredients for the cake batter ,the semolina flour, yoghurt, sugar, melted ghee, coconut flakes, baking powder, vanilla and salt.
3. Mix until barely just combined. Do not over mix or your cake will be tough.
4. Tap the cake pan gently on the table to ensure there are no cake bubbles present and everything is even.
5. Bake on the center rack of the oven for 10 minutes.
6. Move the pan to the top rack and bake for an additional 10-15 minutes, or until the center of the cake is set and it is starting to turn golden brown.
7. During the last 10-15 minutes, prepare the simple syrup. Combine the sugar and water and in a small saucepan and bring to a boil. Reduce heat to a simmer and allow simmering for 10 minutes.
8. When the cake is done, remove from oven and turn the oven off.
9. Immediately pour the hot syrup over the hot cake.
10. Cover the pan with foil and allow sitting for at least 1 hour to soak in the syrup.
11. Slice and enjoy!

Serving Suggestion: Serve warm slices.
Variation Tip: You can flavor the simple syrup using either 2 teaspoons vanilla extract, 2 teaspoons orange blossom water, 2 teaspoons rose water, or ½ of a cinnamon stick.
Nutritional Information per Serving:
Calories 350|Carbohydrates 45g|Protein 6g|Fat 13g|Sodium 284mg|Fiber 2g

Sorcerer's Steak and Kidney Pie

Prep Time: 10 minutes|Cook Time: 30 minutes|Servings: 8

Ingredients:

For the dough:

2½ cups plain flour
1 teaspoon salt
1 cup unsalted butter, chilled

¼ cup water
1 tablespoon butter, melted

For the filling:

1-pound chuck steak, browned
½ teaspoon cayenne pepper

½ cup red wine
½ teaspoon salt
2 lamb kidneys, pan-fried

Preparation:

1. Preheat the oven to 400°F.
2. Spray a pie pan with cooking oil.
3. Put the flour, salt, and butter in a bowl. Mix well.
4. Slowly add water and mix until a dough that's not too sticky forms.
5. Split the dough in half, one half for the base of the pie and one for the top, and set aside.
6. Chop up the beef and lamb kidneys. Mix together in a bowl.
7. Sprinkle the meat with salt and cayenne pepper.
8. Spread one dough half over the bottom and up the sides of the pie pan and place the mixture in the center.
9. Add the red wine.
10. Place the other half of the dough on top. Press the edges of the dough halves together.
11. Brush some melted butter on top.
12. Bake for about 30 minutes or until golden.
13. Serve and enjoy!

Serving Suggestions: Serve alongside fresh greens.
Variation Tip: Add some minced garlic when cooking the beef.
Nutritional Information per Serving:
Calories: 386|Fat: 21.15g|Sat Fat: 12.22g|Carbohydrates: 29.97g|Fiber: 1.1g|Sugar: 0.12g|Protein: 18.18g

Magical Bangers and Mash

Prep Time: 15 minutes|Cook Time: 45 minutes|Servings: 8

Ingredients

8 large baking potatoes, peeled and quartered
2 teaspoons butter, divided
½ cup milk, or as needed
salt and pepper to taste

1½ pounds beef sausage
½ cup diced onion
1 (0.75-ounce) packet dry brown gravy mix
1 cup water, or as needed

Preparations

1. Preheat the oven to 350°F.
2. Place potatoes in a saucepan with enough water to cover. Bring to a boil, and cook until tender, about 20 minutes. Drain, and mash with 1 teaspoon of butter, and enough milk to reach your desired creaminess. Continue mashing, or beat with an electric mixer, until smooth. Season with salt and pepper.
3. In a large skillet over medium heat, cook the sausage until heated through. Remove from pan, and set aside. Add remaining teaspoon of butter to the skillet, and fry the onions over medium heat until tender. Mix gravy mix and water as directed on the package, and add to the skillet with the onions. Simmer, stirring constantly, to form a thick gravy.
4. Pour half of the gravy into a square casserole dish so that it coats the bottom. Place sausages in the layer over the gravy (you can butterfly the sausages if you wish). Pour remaining gravy over them, then top with mashed potatoes.
5. Bake uncovered for 20 minutes in the preheated oven, or until potatoes are evenly brown.

Serving Suggestion: Serve hot topped with freshly chopped chives.
Variation Tip: Add chili flakes for spiciness.
Nutritional Information Per Serving:
Calories 420|Carbohydrates 33.9g|Protein 10.2g|Fat 28.4g|Sodium 435mg|Fiber 2.9g

Marvelous Mashed Potatoes with Gravy

Prep Time: 30 minutes|Cook Time: 50 minutes|Servings: 4

Ingredients:

6 medium potatoes, peeled
2 tablespoons salt
4 tablespoons unsalted butter
1 cup whole milk or half-and-half
½ teaspoon ground black pepper
¼ teaspoon ground nutmeg

3 tablespoons vegetable oil
1 medium yellow onion, finely diced
3 tablespoons all-purpose flour
2 cups vegetable broth
Salt, to taste

Preparation:

1. Put the potatoes in a pot with water over high heat.
2. Bring the pot to a boil and cook the potatoes for 20 minutes.
3. Drain the potatoes.
4. Put the boiled potatoes, salt, butter, milk, black pepper, and nutmeg in a large bowl.
5. Mash the potatoes using a fork until everything is mixed properly.
6. To make the gravy, heat the oil in a pan over medium heat.
7. Add the onions and cook until golden.
8. Stir in the flour and mix well.
9. Now, add in the broth. Whisk together until you have a thick gravy.
10. Serve the mashed potatoes on a plate with the onion gravy on top.
11. Enjoy!

Serving Suggestions: Serve with one or two sausages.
Variation Tip: Use unsweetened non-dairy milk.
Nutritional Information per Serving:
Calories: 670|Fat: 20.44g|Sat Fat: 14.38g|Carbohydrates: 111.17g|Fiber: 12.5g|Sugar: 13.47g|Protein: 14.18g

Christmas Broccoli Casserole

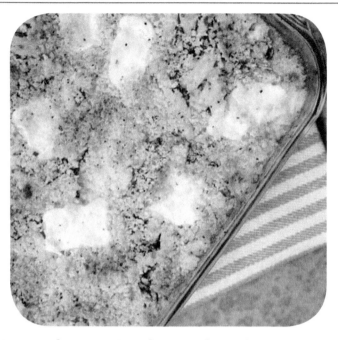

Prep Time: 10 minutes|Cook Time: 45 minutes|Servings: 10

Ingredients

6 cups fresh broccoli florets
1 (10.5 ounces) can cream of mushroom soup
1 cup mayonnaise
2 large eggs
2 tablespoons dried minced

onion
1 cup freshly grated sharp cheddar cheese
1 cup cheese crackers, crushed

Preparation

1. Bring a large pot of water to a boil. Boil broccoli for 2 minutes. Drain well.
2. In a large mixing bowl, combine mushroom soup, mayonnaise, eggs, onions and shredded cheese and mix well.
3. Pour over broccoli and toss to combine. Pour into greased casserole dish.
4. Sprinkle crushed cheese crackers on top.
5. Bake at 400°F for 40 to 45 minutes.

Serving Suggestion: Serve warm along with poly juice potion.
Variation Tip: Allow to it come to room temperature for 20 minutes before adding cheese crackers and baking.
Nutritional Information Per Serving:
Calories 277|Carbohydrates 9g|Protein 7g|Fat 23g|Sodium 512mg|Fiber 1g

Roast Chicken with Gravy

Prep Time: 20 minutes|Cook Time: 100 minutes|Servings: 4

Ingredients

For the chicken:

1 (5-pound) whole chicken	butter, cut into small pieces
1 tablespoon unsalted butter, melted	kosher salt, to taste
1 tablespoon cold unsalted	freshly ground black pepper, to taste

For the stuffing:

¼ cup unsalted butter	fresh parsley
½ cup coarsely chopped onion	2 cups soft breadcrumbs
½ cup coarsely chopped celery	⅔ cup milk, divided
½ teaspoon dried thyme	kosher salt, to taste
2 tablespoons finely chopped	freshly ground black pepper, to taste
	1 large egg, beaten

For the pan gravy:

drippings from the chicken	flour
3 tablespoons all-purpose	1½ to 2 cups chicken stock

Preparation

1. Preheat the oven to 375°F. Line a roasting pan with foil.
2. Rub chicken with the cold melted butter. Tuck the pieces of cold butter under the chicken's skin along with the optional fresh herbs. Sprinkle the chicken generously with salt and pepper. Set aside while making the stuffing.
3. Melt the butter in a skillet or sauté pan over medium-low heat. Add the chopped onion and celery. Cook, stirring, for about 5 minutes, or until the onion is translucent and the celery is crisp-tender.
4. Add the dried thyme, parsley, and breadcrumbs. Add about ⅓ cup of milk and stir to blend. Taste and season the stuffing with salt and pepper.
5. Stir in the beaten egg and enough of the remaining ⅓ cup of milk, if needed, one tablespoon at a time to make a moist mixture. Remove from heat.
6. Loosely spoon the stuffing into the cavity of the chicken.
7. Close the cavity by sewing the loose skin together with toothpicks, or twine. Alternatively, cover the cavity with a piece of foil or a slice of bread.
8. Place the chicken, breast side up, on the rack in the roasting pan.
9. Roast the whole chicken in the preheated oven for about 1 hour and 30 minutes to 1 hour and 45 minutes, basting several times with the pan juices.
10. When done, the internal temperature of the thickest part of the thigh, away from fat and bone must read the minimum safe temperature for consumption of 165°F.
11. Once cooked thoroughly, remove from the oven and let rest for about 15 minutes.
12. For Gravy: Skim off the fat from the pan drippings, or use a fat separator. Reserve the fat.
13. Add three tablespoons of fat back in the roasting pan, reserving the remaining drippings. Add the flour and stir to make a roux. Cook on the stove, stirring, for two minutes.
14. Put the reserved drippings in a 2-cup measuring cup and add enough chicken stock until you have 2 full cups of liquid.
15. Gradually stir the chicken stock mixture into the roux mixture. Continue cooking the gravy until thickened, stirring constantly. Season with salt and pepper to taste.

Serving Suggestion: Serve chicken topped with gravy alongside with mashed potatoes.

Variation Tip: Use sweet seasoning if you have a s sweet tooth.

Nutritional Information Per Serving:
Calories 101.7|Carbohydrates 8.3g|Protein 11.3g|Fat 2.3g|Sodium 433.3mg|Fiber 0.8g

Lestrange's Creamy Lasagna

Prep Time: 30 minutes|Cook Time: 45 minutes- 30 minutes cooling time|Servings: 12

Ingredients:

9 lasagna noodles cooked al dente

4 cups shredded rotisserie chicken or cooked from 2 pounds chicken breast

Spinach Cream Sauce:

1 tablespoon olive oil

1 medium onion finely chopped

4 tablespoons unsalted butter

⅓ cup all-purpose flour

2 ½ cups chicken broth

1 ½ cups equal parts of heavy cream and milk

5 ounces fresh spinach coarsely chopped

2 teaspoons sea salt

½ teaspoon black pepper

3 garlic cloves minced

Ricotta Cheese Sauce:

15 ounces ricotta

1 large egg

¼ cup parsley

¼ cup Parmesan cheese

3 cups Mozzarella cheese, divided

Preparation:

1. Preheat oven to 375° F.

2. Cook pasta in a large pot of salted water until al dente according to package directions then drain hot water and add cold water to the pot to stop the cooking process and prevent noodles from sticking together.

3. Shred 4 cups of chicken.

4. Place a pot or large saucepan over medium heat; add 1 tablespoon olive oil and sauté onions for 3-4 minutes or until softened.

5. Add 4 tablespoons butter and whisk in ⅓ cup flour. Continue whisking 3 minutes or until flour mixture is golden.

6. Add 2 ½ cups chicken broth, 1 ½ cups half and half, 2 teaspoon salt and ½ teaspoon black pepper.

7. Whisk until smooth and simmer 5 minutes until thickened to a light gravy consistency.

8. Add minced garlic and chopped spinach, and stir to combine then remove from heat.

9. In a large bowl, whisk together: Ricotta, egg, 2 cups Mozzarella cheese, ¼ cup Parmesan, and ¼ cup parsley.

10. Add a little bechamel sauce on the bottom of a 9x13 casserole dish, add 3 noodles, Add ½ ricotta sauce, ½ shredded chicken then ladle ⅓ of spinach sauce over the chicken.

11. Add 3 noodles, ½ Ricotta cheese, ½ shredded chicken, and ⅓ spinach sauce

12. Add 3 noodles, remaining ⅓ sauce, and sprinkle on reserved 1 cup cheese.

13. Arrange 10-12 toothpicks over the top to keep the foil from touching the cheese then cover with a large sheet of foil.

14. Bake on the center rack in a preheated oven at 375° F for 45 minutes then uncover and broil 2-3 minutes to brown the cheese.

15. Rest at least 10 minutes uncovered before slicing.

Serving Suggestion: Serve warm with chilled beer.
Variation Tip: Add chopped thyme and dill for flavor.
Nutritional Information per Serving:
Calories 337|Carbohydrates 24g|Protein 18g|Fat 19g|Sodium 670mg|Fiber 1g

Peppermint Pork Pies

Prep Time: 10 minutes|Cook Time: 55 minutes|Servings: 24

Ingredients

¾ pound ground pork

1 large sweet or yellow onion, small diced

2 tablespoons butter

1¼ cups water

1 teaspoon gunpowder tea

2 teaspoons dried peppermint

2 teaspoons dried mint leaves

½ tablespoon sugar

4 cups all-purpose flour

2 teaspoons table salt

1 cup lard, shredded

½ cup milk

1 egg, beaten

kosher salt

Preparation

Make the tea:

1. Add the tea leaves to the infuser. Bring the water to a boil in the kettle and pour it into a measuring cup. Lower in the infuser and let steep for approximately 3 minutes.

2. Remove the infuser and set the tea aside. You should have about 1 cup of tea.

Make the filling:

1. Heat the butter in the medium pot over medium-low heat until hot. Stir in the onion and cover the pot with the lid. Cook occasionally stirring, until softened.

2. Deglaze the pan with ½ cup of tea, pour in the sugar, and season with kosher salt.

3. Continue cooking while scraping the browned bits from the pan for another 3 to 5 minutes or until the liquid is fully absorbed.

4. Scrape the onions into a mixing bowl and stir in the dried mint leaves and another pinch or two of kosher salt.

5. Fold in the ground pork until thoroughly incorporated.

Cover the bowl and place it in the refrigerator to chill while making the crust.

Make the crust:

1. Whisk flour and table salt together in a large, heat-resistant bowl. Spray each cup in the muffin pan with baking spray and set aside.

2. Clean out the pan you used to caramelize the onion. Pour in the remaining tea, the milk, and the lard. Set it on the stovetop over medium heat.

3. Set a separate kettle with extra water to boil.

4. Stir the contents of the saucepan. When the mixture just comes to a boil, immediately pour it into the flour mixture and blend with a spatula or wooden spoon until a dough form.

5. Add extra hot water from the kettle if the dough is too dry, extra flour if too wet, until it's workable enough to roll.

Make the pies:

1. Preheat the oven to 325°F. Pour a little of the boiling water into the other heat-resistant bowl and place the dough bowl into it to keep it warm.

2. Divide the dough into six portions. Take out a portion and cover the bowl.

3. Roll the portion out on a lightly floured surface and cut circles with the 3-inch biscuit cutter. Gently roll each circle a little larger and then use them to line the cups of the muffin tin. Repeat until each cup is lined.

4. Drop a tablespoon of pork filling into each cup.

5. Roll and cut lids for the pies using a 2-inch cutter. Roll the circles slightly larger, the poke and round out a hole in the center of each lid using a chopstick. Place a lid on top of each pie, pressing the pastry together and crimping closed.

6. Glaze each pie with a beaten egg using a pastry brush and bake in the oven 40 to 45 minutes or until golden.

7. Let them cool for at least 5 minutes before serving.

Serving Suggestion: Serve cold with hot tea.

Variation Tip: Add mushrooms along the pork.

Nutritional Information Per Serving:

Calories 125|Carbohydrates 7.1g|Protein 2.8g|Fat 9.5g|Sodium 169mg|Fiber 1g

Juicy Pork Loin Roast

Prep Time: 15 minutes|Cook Time: 1 hour|Servings: 8

Ingredients:

For the pork loin:
3 pounds pork loin   1 tablespoon olive oil

For the Spice Rub:
1 teaspoon sweet paprika   ½ teaspoon dried rosemary
1 teaspoon garlic powder   Salt and fresh ground pepper,
½ teaspoon onion powder   to taste
½ teaspoon dried thyme

For the Honey Garlic Glaze:
4 cloves garlic, minced   gluten free soy sauce
¼ cup honey   1 tablespoon Dijon mustard
3 tablespoons low-sodium   1 tablespoon olive oil

For the vegetables:
1 tablespoon olive oil   1 pound butternut squash,
1 pound brussels sprouts, cut   peeled, seeds cleaned out,
in half   and cut into 1-inch cubes

Preparation:

1. Preheat oven to 375° F. Line a rimmed baking sheet with aluminum foil or parchment paper and set aside. Pat dry pork loin with paper towels.

2. In a small mixing bowl combine paprika, garlic powder, onion powder, thyme, rosemary, salt and pepper.

3. Lightly spray pork loin with cooking spray. This will make it easier for the spice mix to stick.

4. Take the spice mix and rub it all over the pork loin.

5. Heat olive oil over medium heat and sear the pork loin until browned on all sides; about 3 to 5 minutes per side. Transfer pork loin to previously prepare baking sheet, fat-layer side up; set aside.

6. In a bowl, combine garlic, honey, soy sauce, mustard and oil; whisk until well combined. If too thick, add a bit more oil or soy sauce. Reserve 2 tablespoons of the sauce to use for the vegetables.

7. Brush remaining honey mixture over the pork loin. Roast for 25 minutes.

8. In the meantime, toss the vegetables with a tbsp of olive oil and the reserved honey mixture. Pull pork roast out of the oven and add the vegetables all around it in one layer.

9. Tent a piece of foil over the pork so the top doesn't burn, but the inside continues to cook. Put back in the oven and continue to cook for 25 to 30 more minutes, or until internal temperature of the pork loin reaches 145° F. Use an Instant Read Thermometer to check for doneness. Stir vegetables half way through cooking.

10. Remove baking sheet from oven and loosely cover meat and veggies with foil; let rest 10 minutes..

Serving Suggestion: Cut the pork in slices and serve with veggies.

Variation Tip: Add your favorite veggies and mashed potatoes as a side.

Nutritional Information per Serving:
Calories 347|Carbohydrates 22g|Protein 41g|Fat 11g|Sodium 322mg|Fiber 4g

Beef & Apple Pasties

Prep Time: 10 minutes|Cook Time: 55 minutes|Servings: 24 mini pasties

Ingredients

1 large yellow onion, small diced

1 large apple, cored and small diced

¾ pound ground beef

2 tablespoons unsalted butter

1 cup strongly brewed tea

1 tablespoon sugar

4 ounces blue cheese crumbles

4 cups all-purpose flour

½ cup milk

2 teaspoons table salt

1 cup lard, shredded

1 egg, beaten

kosher salt

Preparation

Make the Filling:

1. Brown and break the ground beef into crumbles in the skillet on the stovetop over medium heat. Scrape the meat into a mixing bowl.

2. Drain off half of the fat in a disposable container to discard, or into a sealable container for later use.

3. Reduce the heat to medium low. Melt the butter in the skillet with the remaining fat. Add the apple and onion and cook covered, 15 to 18 minutes. Stir occasionally, until they start sticking to the bottom of the pan.

4. Deglaze the pan with a ½ cup of tea. Stir in the sugar, and season with kosher salt.

5. Continue cooking while scraping the browned bits from the pan for another 3 to 5 minutes or until the liquid is fully absorbed.

6. Scrape the onions and apple into the mixing bowl and combine with the beef and a pinch or two of kosher salt. Chill the filling in the refrigerator until you are ready to assemble the pies.

Make the Crust:

1. Preheat the oven to 325°F.

2. Whisk flour and table salt together in a large, heat-resistant bowl.

3. Pour the remaining tea, the milk, and the lard into the saucepan over medium heat on the stovetop. Turn on the tea kettle with more water to boil.

4. Stir the contents of the saucepan. As soon as the mixture comes to a boil, immediately pour it into the flour mixture. Mix with a spatula or wooden spoon until a dough forms.

5. Add extra hot water from the kettle if the dough is too dry; add extra flour if too wet, until it's workable enough to roll.

Make the Pies:

1. Pour a little the boiling water into the baking dish and place the dough bowl into it to keep it warm

2. Divide the dough into six portions. Take out a portion and cover the bowl. Roll the portion out on a lightly floured surface and cut circles with a 3-inch biscuit cutter. Gently roll each circle a little larger.

3. Drop a tablespoon of pie filling onto half of each circle. Fold the pastry over the filling and press the edges together to seal.

4. Cut a corner of the border and roll the edge. Place each finished pie on a parchment paper-lined baking sheet and glaze with beaten egg.

5. Repeat until you run out of dough.

6. Bake the pies 30 to 45 minutes or until golden.

7. Let the pies cool at least five minutes before handling.

Serving Suggestion: Serve warm with tea.
Variation Tip: Add veggies to pie.
Nutritional Information Per Serving:
Calories 594|Carbohydrates 78.4g|Protein 5.8g|Fat 31.1g|Sodium 430.3mg|Fiber 7.5g

Apple Glazed Pork Tenderloin

Prep Time: 15 minutes|Cook Time: 30 minutes|Servings: 4

Ingredients:

1 tablespoon olive oil
1 (1 ¼ pound) pork tenderloin
Kosher salt and ground black pepper to taste
2 teaspoon chopped fresh parsley
½ sweet onion, diced
1 Gala apple, cut into chunks
½ cup Riesling wine
1 cup apple jelly
2 tablespoons Balsamic vinegar

Preparation:

1. Preheat an oven to 350°F .Grease a baking dish large enough to hold the tenderloin without folding it.
2. Heat the olive oil in a large skillet over medium-high heat, and brown the pork tenderloin on all sides. Remove the browned tenderloin to the prepared baking dish. Sprinkle all sides of the meat with salt, pepper, and parsley.
3. Cook and stir the onion and apple in the same skillet over medium heat until the onion becomes soft, about 5 minutes, and pour in the Riesling wine. Scrape all the browned flavor bits off the bottom of the skillet and stir to help dissolve them into the wine. Bring to a boil, and pour the onion, apple, and wine mixture over the tenderloin.
4. Mix together the apple jelly and balsamic vinegar in a bowl until the mixture is smooth and without lumps. Spread the jelly mixture all over the pork.
5. Bake loin in the preheated oven until an instant-read thermometer inserted into the center reads 145°F , 30 to 45 minutes. Allow the tenderloin to rest for 10 minutes before slicing.

Serving Suggestion: Serve each slice with a spoonful of the apple-onion mixture.
Variation Tip: Add mashed potatoes.
Nutritional Information per Serving:
Calories 434|Carbohydrates 65g|Protein 22g|Fat 6.4g|Sodium 154mg|Fiber 2g

Yule Ball Pork Chops

Prep Time: 10 minutes|Cook Time: 30 minutes|Servings: 12

Ingredients

2 tablespoons all-purpose flour
¼ teaspoon salt
a pinch of pepper
¾ cup bread crumbs
½ cup grated parmesan cheese
1½ teaspoons rubbed sage
½ teaspoon grated lemon peel
1 egg, lightly beaten
4 bone-in pork loin chops
1 tablespoon olive or vegetable oil
1 tablespoon butter

Preparation

1. In a shallow dish, combine the flour, salt and pepper.
2. In another shallow dish, combine the bread crumbs, parmesan cheese, sage and lemon peel. Place egg in shallow bowl.
3. Coat the pork chops with flour mixture, dip them into the egg, then coat with breadcrumb mixture. Let them rest for 5 minutes.
4. In a skillet, brown the chops in oil and butter for 2 minutes on each side. Transfer to a greased 11-inch-by-7-inch-by-2-inch baking dish.
5. Bake uncovered at 425°F for 10 to 15 minutes or until juices run clear.

Serving Suggestion: Serve with rice.
Variation Tip: Add sauté mushroom for a side dish.
Nutritional Information Per Serving:
Calories 175.7|Carbohydrates 0.3g|Protein 23.8g|Fat 8.1g|Sodium 67.5mg|Fiber 0.1g

Dragon Tartare

Prep Time: 30 minutes|Cook Time: 30 minutes|Servings: 4

Ingredients

For "tartare":

24 ounces flank steak	½ cup plain bread crumbs
1 cup mushrooms, finely chopped	2 tablespoons butter, for greasing and sautéing
4 cloves black garlic, roughly chopped	salt & pepper, to taste
3 shallots, finely chopped	fresh parsley, chopped for topping
3 slices thick cut bacon	red pepper flakes, for topping
1 tablespoon horseradish	to taste
1 egg	

For chanterelle & black garlic mash:

4 chanterelle mushrooms, roughly chopped	1 chili pepper, chopped
1 head black garlic, chopped	4 teaspoons fresh thyme on stem
½ cup butter	1 teaspoon horseradish

salt & pepper, to taste

Preparation

1. In a skillet over medium heat, melt butter until frothy. Add the minced chanterelle, shallots and black garlic cloves. Sauté until fragrant, about 2 to 3 minutes.

2. Remove from the pan, set aside and wipe the pan clean.

3. Preheat the oven to 425°F. In the same skillet over medium high heat, fry the bacon slices until crispy, about 5 to 6 minutes.

4. Remove the bacon from the pan but reserve the grease. Finely chop the cooked bacon. (No larger than an inch)

5. In a large bowl stir together the bread crumbs, egg, horseradish, bacon grease, bacon bits and the sautéed chanterelles, shallots and black garlic.

6. Stir in the raw meat until coated in the crumb. Season with salt and pepper to taste.

7. Grease 4 ramekins with the remaining butter. Tightly pack the meat mixture into the ramekins.

8. Bake for 10 to 15 minutes, until the internal temperature reaches 145°F. They will continue to cook after being removed from the oven.

9. While the meat is cooking, melt the half cup of butter in a large skillet.

10. Add the chopped chanterelles, black garlic, Chile pepper, horseradish and thyme. Keep the thyme on the stem.

11. Sauté over low heat until the chanterelles are golden brown, about 10 to 15 minutes. Remove the thyme from the skillet. Season with salt and pepper, to taste.

12. Let the ramekins rest for 10 minutes prior to turning out the meat stacks.

Serving Suggestion: Top with the chanterelle and black garlic mash.

Variation Tip: Finish the meat stacks with a brulee torch as desired.

Nutritional Information Per Serving:
Calories 186|Carbohydrates 23g|Protein 17g|Fat 12g|Sodium 61mg|Fiber 2g

Cheddar Pumpkin Pasties

Prep Time: 20 minutes|Cook Time: 30 minutes|Servings: 4

Ingredients

½ medium-sized pumpkin	salt and pepper, to taste
4 tablespoons butter	1 pie crust
1 clove garlic, minced	flour, for dusting
½ cup shredded white cheddar cheese	heavy cream or egg wash, for brushing

Preparations:
1. Preheat oven to 400°F. Place parchment paper on 2 half-sheet pans.
2. Scoop the inside of the pumpkin into a large bowl. Mash it with butter. Stir in garlic and cheddar cheese and season with salt and pepper to taste.
3. Thaw pie dough according to package directions.
4. Dust a large, flat surface with flour. Roll pie crust out to ⅛-inch thick and cut 4 circles. Reroll scraps if necessary.
5. Spoon about ½ cup of the pumpkin mixture onto the center of each circle. Fold the pie dough over the filling to create half-moons. Use the side of your hand to press the dough ends together, leaving about a ½-inch border.
6. Use a fork to firmly seal the dough and for decorative crimping. Use a sharp paring knife to cut 3 slivers on the tops of the pies for ventilation.
7. Transfer pies to baking tray and coat with heavy cream or egg wash and bake for 25 to 30 minutes until pie crust turns golden brown.
8. Transfer to a cooling rack and let it rest for at least 5 to 10 minutes before serving.

Serving Suggestion: Serve with your favorite sides and drinks.
Variation Tip: Use 2 sweet potatoes instead of pumpkin.
Nutritional Information Per Serving:
Calories 142|Carbohydrates 20.4g|Protein 1.2g|Fat 5.7g|Sodium 139.4mg|Fiber 0.5g

Lemony Drumsticks

Prep Time: 15 minutes|Cook Time: 30 minutes|Servings: 4

Ingredients:

8 chicken drumsticks	2 tablespoons lemon juice
2 tablespoons unsalted butter	Salt and pepper
1 clove garlic, chopped	

Preparation:
1. Preheat the oven over 350°F.
2. Melt butter with garlic and lemon juice over medium-low heat.
3. Season drumsticks with salt and pepper. Brush each lightly with lemon butter. Bake for 20 minutes.
4. Position oven rack about 8 inches from heat source. Preheat broiler; line a broiling pan with foil. Pat drumsticks dry and trim off fat. Arrange in a single layer on prepared pan.
5. Broil, turning often and brushing with lemon butter, until chicken is browned and crisp and has no traces of pink juices when pierced, about 30 minutes. Cool slightly.

Serving Suggestion: Serve drumsticks with dipping sauces.
Variation Tip: Add herbs for the flavor .
Nutritional Information per Serving:
Calories 279|Carbohydrates 1g|Protein 28g|Fat 17g|Sodium 95mg|Fiber 0g

Haggis Stacks

Prep Time: 30 minutes|Cook Time: 1 hour 10 minutes|Servings: 6

Ingredients

1 can haggis, sliced or crumbled
1 loaf peasant bread, sliced thick
1 large turnip, chopped
1 head garlic

1 potato, chopped
2 tablespoons olive oil
1 cup mushrooms, sliced
1 teaspoon red pepper flakes
salt & pepper, to taste

Preparation

1. Preheat the oven to 375°F. Arrange the chopped turnips and garlic head on a baking sheet and drizzle with olive oil. Bake for 30 to 40 minutes until roasted tender. Remove the garlic cloves from the paper while the head is still warm. Keep oven on.
2. Meanwhile on the stove, bring a medium pot of water to a rolling boil. Boil the potatoes until tender, about 30 to 40 minutes. Drain.
3. Sauté the sliced mushrooms until they've softened and browned, about 10 minutes. Stir in the red pepper flakes. Season with salt and pepper to taste. Remove from the skillet but do not clean the skillet.
4. Crumble the haggis, as desired. Use the same skillet to cook the mushrooms and sauté haggis until it is heated through about 3 to 5 minutes. Remove from heat.
5. In a large bowl, mash together the turnips, garlic and potatoes. Season with salt and pepper, to taste.
6. Slice the bread into thick slices. Spread on about 1 to 2 tablespoon of the mash then top with the haggis and finally mushrooms.

7. Arrange the stacks on a baking sheet. Bake in the preheated oven until heated through about 10 minutes.

Serving Suggestion: Serve warm and enjoy with a Harry Potter movie.
Variation Tip: Sweet potato mash also goes well with it.
Nutritional Information Per Serving:
Calories 518|Carbohydrates 76g|Protein 10g|Fat 22g|Sodium 303mg|Fiber 11g

Magical Honey Baked Chicken

Prep Time: 5 minutes|Cook Time: 1 hour 15 minutes|Servings: 5

Ingredients:

⅓ cup butter, melted
⅓ cup honey
2 tablespoons mustard
1 teaspoon salt
1 teaspoon curry powder

3 pound chicken (legs, thighs, or any combo of chicken with skin and bone still attached)

Preparation:

1. Preheat oven to 350°F.
2. In a small bowl, whisk the butter, honey, mustard, salt and curry.
3. Arrange chicken pieces into a baking dish.
4. Pour the sauce over the chicken and place the pan in the oven.
5. Bake for approximately 1 hour 15 minutes, basting the chicken with the sauce every 15 minutes.

Serving Suggestion: Serve warm with cold butter beer.
Variation Tip: Add thyme as flavor enhancer.
Nutritional Information per Serving:
Calories 837|Carbohydrates 19g|Protein 76g|Fat 54g|Sodium 881mg|Fiber 0g

Cornish Pasties

Prep Time: 30 minutes|Cook Time: 45 minutes|Servings: 12

Ingredients
Crust

4 cups all-purpose flour	2 rutabagas, diced
1 teaspoon salt	1 pound lean ground beef
2 cups lard	1 pound ground pork
1 cup cold water	10 green onions, chopped
3 tablespoons vegetable oil	salt and pepper to taste
1 onion, finely diced	½ cup butter
5 carrots, diced (optional)	2 tablespoons milk

Preparation
1. To make crust. Place flour and salt in a large bowl. Mix well, and then cut in lard until mixture is crumbly.
2. Stir in water, mixing just until dough forms a ball. Allow dough to rest in refrigerator while you make filling.
3. Heat a large skillet over medium-high heat. Add vegetable oil, then onions. Sauté vegetables until soft, taking about 10 minutes.
4. Add ground beef, ground pork, and green onions to skillet. Sauté until meat is no longer pink. Add salt and pepper to taste.
5. Preheat the oven to 400°F.
6. Divide the dough into 12 portions and roll out each one to fit a 9-inch pie plate.
7. Place a pastry circle in a pie pan. Fill one half of pan with meat filling.
8. Dot with some of the butter. Pat edge of crust with water, and then fold over other half of the crust.
9. Trim edge, then crimp to seal. Make steam vents by piercing the top of the crust with a fork. Brush with milk.
10. Bake in the preheated oven for 45 minutes or until crust is golden brown.

Serving Suggestion: Serve warm with butter beer.
Variation Tip: Use chicken and turkey instead of pork and beef.
Nutritional Information Per Serving:
Calories 800|Carbohydrates 41g|Protein 18.9g|Fat 61.8g|Sodium 330.2mg|Fiber 5g

Kreacher's French Onion Soup Recipe

Prep Time: 30 minutes|Cook Time: 30 minutes|Servings: 2

Ingredients:
Croutons:

Butter	¼ cup grated cheese
1 small baguette, sliced	(Parmesan preferred)

French Onion Soup:

1 tablespoon butter	1 tablespoon plain flour
2 onions	2.5 cups beef stock
Pinch of salt	¼ cup red wine
Pinch of black pepper	1 teaspoon thyme
Pinch of sugar	1 bay leaf

Preparation:
1. Peel onions and finely slice into thin strips.
2. Preheat oven to 350°F. Butter slices of baguette, sprinkle with grated cheese and grill until lightly browned.
3. In a saucepan, melt butter and sauté the onions for a few minutes. Sprinkle with salt and pepper, then add in sugar and continue to cook until browned.
4. Sprinkle the flour in, and then stir in the beef stock and red wine. Toss in the thyme and bay leaf, and then bring to a simmer.
5. Cook for 30 minutes, and then serve with the grilled baguette slices.

Serving Suggestion: Serve with the grilled baguette slices.
Variation Tip: Can also go best with garlic bread.
Nutritional Information per Serving:
Calories 165.9|Carbohydrates 14.7g|Protein 14.6g|Fat 6.1g|Sodium 107mg|Fiber 2.0g

Shell Cottage Pâté Chinois

Prep Time: 20 minutes|Cook Time: 2 hour|Servings: 4

Ingredients

16 ounces ground beef or lamb or veal

½ cup white onion, chopped

½ cup tomato, chopped

½ cup green bell pepper, chopped

2 whole carrots, chopped

2 tablespoons garlic, minced

2 ribs celery, chopped

1 tablespoon thyme

1 tablespoon fresh parsley, chopped

6 ounces tomato paste

¼ cup flour

2 cups beef broth

½ cup cooking sherry

1 teaspoon Worcestershire sauce

1 teaspoon paprika

1 teaspoon chicken base

2 teaspoons balsamic vinegar

1 package garlic mashed potatoes

2 tablespoons butter

salt & pepper, to taste

Preparation

1. Brown the meat in a large pot over medium-high heat. Once browned and crumbled, remove the meat from the pot and drain in a colander. Rinse with cold water.

2. Without washing the skillet, add the white onion and sautéed for 3 to 5 minutes or until it has started to soften. Then add the peppers, celery, carrots and garlic. Sauté for another 5 minutes or until the carrots are tender.

3. Stir in the tomatoes and sauté until they've started to lose their moisture. Scatter the flour over the vegetables and stir until the vegetables are coated in flour.

4. Stir in the tomato paste until a thick, sticky mass of vegetables forms. Deglaze the pan with the cooking sherry and scrape up the brown bits.

5. Pour in the beef broth, Worcestershire sauce, and paprika, chicken base and balsamic vinegar. Season with salt and pepper, to taste.

6. Add the meat back to the pot and stir it all together. Simmer for 20 to 30 minutes, or until most of the liquid has evaporated off.

7. Preheat the oven to 400°F. Spoon the meat mixture into the baking dish or individual ramekins.

8. Dollop the mashed potatoes on top of the meat and use the back of the spoon to spread the potatoes into an even layer.

9. Bake in the oven for 30 minutes and then broil on high for 5 to 10 additional minutes until the top is sufficiently browned and crisp. Let it set for 5 to 10 minute prior to serving.

Serving Suggestion: Serve warm.

Variation Tip: Use chopped chives for freshness.

Nutritional Information Per Serving:

Calories 312|Carbohydrates 25g|Protein 27g|Fat 10g|Sodium 581mg|Fiber 2g

Sheet Pan Sausage and Vegetables

Prep Time: 25 minutes|Cook Time: 25 minutes|Servings: 4

Ingredients

1 large red onion, halved and sliced	1 teaspoon salt
3 large carrots, sliced	½ teaspoon freshly ground black pepper
1 pound Brussels sprouts, stemmed and halved	1 teaspoon dried thyme
3 tablespoons extra virgin olive oil	1 pound fresh hot Italian sausage

Preparation

1. Preheat the oven to 425°F and set the oven rack in the middle position.
2. Line a 13-inch-by-18-inch baking tray with heavy-duty aluminum foil for easy clean-up.
3. Toss the onion, carrots, and Brussels sprouts, oil, salt, pepper, and thyme onto the tray until the vegetables are evenly coated.
4. Place the sausages on the baking sheet, spacing them evenly around the pan, and arrange the vegetables as best you can in a single layer.
5. Roast for 25 minutes, until the sausages are cooked through and the vegetables are caramelized and tender.

Serving Suggestion: Serve cold topped with butterscotch sauce drizzling.
Variation Tip: Feel free to substitute different vegetables, such as baby potatoes.
Nutritional Information Per Serving:
Calories 566|Carbohydrates 19g|Protein 21g|Fat 46g|Sodium 891mg|Fiber 6g

Baked Breaded Pork Chops

Prep Time: 10 minutes|Cook Time: 17 minutes|Servings: 4

Ingredients:

4 pork chops boneless center loin, 1" thick	Parmesan cheese
1 egg whisked	1 teaspoon garlic powder
¼ cup flour	Salt and pepper to taste
½ cup Italian breadcrumbs	1 tablespoon olive oil or as needed
2 tablespoons grated	

Preparation:

1. Preheat oven to 425°F and line a rimmed baking sheet with parchment paper.
2. In a shallow bowl combine bread crumbs, Parmesan cheese, garlic powder, and salt and black pepper.
3. Season flour on a shallow plate with salt to taste. In another shallow bowl add the whisked egg.
4. Dab the pork chops dry with a paper towel and lightly dredge in flour. Dip the pork chop into the egg, making sure to coat all sides. Dip the pork chop into the bread crumb mixture.
5. Heat olive oil In a frying pan over medium-high heat. Brown pork chops for 1 minute per side.
6. Add to the prepared baking sheet and bake for about 12-14 minutes or until they reach an internal temperature of 145°F. Do not over bake.
7. Rest 5 minutes before serving

Serving Suggestion: Serve sizzling with chilled butter beer.
Variation Tip: Beef chops are also goes well.
Nutritional Information per Serving:
Calories 471.1|Carbohydrates 15.7g|Protein 59.3g|Fat 17g|Sodium 165.6mg|Fiber 1.9g

Spooky Calzone Snake

Prep Time: 30 minutes|Cook Time: 30 minutes|Servings: 14

Ingredients

Dough

1 teaspoon white sugar	2 tablespoons olive oil
1 cup warm water	1½ teaspoons kosher salt
1 (0.25-ounce) pack active dry yeast	3 cups all-purpose flour, divided

Filling

1 cup ricotta cheese	½ teaspoon Italian seasoning
2 cups shredded mozzarella cheese	½ cup sliced black olives
¼ cup grated parmesan cheese, to taste	½ green bell pepper, cut into strips
1 (4-ounce) pack sliced pepperoni	½ cup sliced fresh mushrooms
1 tablespoon chopped fresh parsley	1 egg
	1 tablespoon water

Preparation

1. Dissolve the sugar in warm water in a bowl. Sprinkle the yeast over the water, and let it stand for 5 minutes until the yeast softens and begins to form creamy foam. Stir in the oil, salt, and 2 cups of flour, and mix until the mixture forms wet dough.

2. Add the last 1 cup of flour, ¼ cup at a time, and knead until the dough pulls away from the sides of the bowl into a ball. Knead, until the dough is smooth and elastic.

3. Lightly oil a large bowl, then place the dough in the bowl and turn to coat with oil. Cover with a light cloth and let it rise in a warm place until doubled in volume, about 1 hour.

4. Combine the ricotta, mozzarella, and parmesan cheese, pepperoni, parsley, Italian seasoning, olives, green pepper, and mushrooms in a large bowl, and set aside.

5. Preheat oven to 375°F. Line a baking tray with parchment paper.

6. Punch down the dough, and roll it out into a long, flat strip about 9 inches wide by 30 inches long.

7. Spoon the filling mixture down the center of the dough strip, leaving about 1 inch on all sides for sealing.

8. Pull edges of the dough together; pinch to seal and form a long, filled roll. Place the roll, seam side down, onto the parchment paper in a snake type "S" shape, and tuck the ends underneath to seal.

9. Beat the egg in a bowl with 1 tablespoon of water, and brush the egg wash over the calzone.

10. Bake in the preheated oven for 30 to 35 minutes, until the calzone is golden brown. Let cool for 5 minutes before cutting into individual slices.

Serving Suggestion: Serve warm with tomato sauce.

Variation Tip: Use fresh boiled vegetable chunks in the filling.

Nutritional Information Per Serving:
Calories 217|Carbohydrates 22.1g|Protein 9.9g|Fat 9.7g|Sodium 512 mg|Fiber 3.1g

Magical Meat Pie

Prep Time: 20 minutes|Cook Time: 40 minutes|Servings: 12

Ingredients

½ pound ground sausage
½ pound ground beef
2 teaspoons minced garlic
2 teaspoons all spice
2 teaspoons dried parsley
1 teaspoon paprika
2 to 3 tablespoons dried

minced onion
2 tablespoons all-purpose flour
1½ cups beef broth
1 cup cubed cooked potatoes
salt and pepper to taste

Crust:

2 cups all-purpose flour
½ teaspoon salt
6 tablespoons cold butter or margarine

6 tablespoons shortening
4 tablespoons cold water
1 egg, plus 2 teaspoon water, beaten

Preparation

1. Combine the flour and salt, cut in the butter and shortening until crumbly. Gradually add water, tossing with a fork until a dough forms and divide into two equal balls. Roll out pastry to fit the pie pan.
2. In a skillet, brown sausage and beef until almost cooked through. Drain the fat.
3. Add spices, garlic, and onion and cook for two more minutes. Add flour and stir.
4. Add broth to the skillet. Bring to a boil and stir in the potatoes. Cook until heated through.
5. Place one crust in bottom of pie pan and trim to ½ inch. Beyond edge of dish, fill with meat mixture.
6. Place second crust on top and press edges of two crusts together and flute edges.
7. Use extra crust to put a fun design on the top of your crust, we did a lightning bolt and the deathly hallows symbol.
8. Brush egg wash on top of crust and prick several times with a fork.
9. Bake at 375°F for 35 to 40 minutes or until pastry is lightly browned on edges.

Serving Suggestion: Serve warm with chilled butter beer.
Variation Tip: Add veggies to the filling if you want veggies.
Nutritional Information Per Serving:

Calories 157|Carbohydrates 9g|Protein 9g|Fat 8g|Sodium 91mg|Fiber 0.1g

Pork Tenderloin with Bourbon-Peach Sauce and Cabbage Slaw

Prep Time: 40 minutes|Cook Time: 40 minutes + 30 minutes cooling time|Servings: 4

Ingredients:

3 tablespoons olive oil, divided
1 pound pork tenderloin, trimmed
1 teaspoon Kosher salt, divided
1 teaspoon black pepper, divided
2 cups sliced peeled fresh peaches
2 tablespoons (1 ounce) bourbon

3 tablespoons apple cider vinegar, divided
2 tablespoons honey, divided
1 tablespoon unsalted butter
1 tablespoon Dijon mustard
3 cups shredded green cabbage (from 1 medium)
½ cup toasted sliced almonds
¼ cup chopped fresh flat-leaf parsley
2 teaspoons finely chopped fresh thyme

Preparation:

1. Heat a large cast-iron skillet over medium-high, and add 1 tablespoon oil. Season pork with ½ teaspoon salt and ½ tsp pepper. Add to skillet, and cook, turning to brown all sides, until a thermometer inserted in thickest portion registers 140°F, 5 to 6 minutes per side. Transfer to a plate.
2. Add peaches to skillet; cook, stirring often, until lightly browned, 2 to 3 minutes. Add bourbon, 1 tablespoon vinegar, and 1 tablespoon honey; cook, stirring often, until sauce is slightly thickened, about 5 minutes. Remove skillet from heat; add butter, swirling until melted.
3. Whisk together mustard, remaining 2 tablespoons oil, remaining 2 tablespoons vinegar, remaining 1 tablespoon honey, remaining ½ teaspoon salt, and remaining ½ teaspoon pepper in a large bowl. Add cabbage, almonds, parsley, and thyme; toss to coat.

Serving Suggestion: Serve Slice pork. Divide slaw and pork among 4 plates; top with peach sauce.
Variation Tip: Add butter beer sauce for buttery flavor.
Nutritional Information per Serving:
Calories 411|Carbohydrates 22g|Protein 28g|Fat 22g|Sodium 643mg|Fiber 4g

Butter Beer Bread

Prep Time: 15 minutes|Cook Time: 40 minutes|Servings: 12

Ingredients:

4 to 4 ½ cups all-purpose flour

1 tablespoon sugar

1 teaspoon salt

1 teaspoon baking soda

4 tablespoons butter

1 cup currants or raisins

1 large egg, lightly beaten

1 ¾ cups buttermilk

Preparation:

1. Preheat oven to 425°F.
2. Whisk together 4 cups of flour, the sugar, salt, and baking soda into a large mixing bowl.
3. Using your clean fingers, work the butter into the flour mixture until it resembles coarse meal, then add in the currants or raisins.
4. Make a well in the center of the flour mixture. Add beaten egg and buttermilk to well and mix in with a wooden spoon until dough is too stiff to stir.
5. Dust hands with a little flour, then gently knead dough in the bowl just long enough to form a rough ball. If the dough is too sticky to work with, add in a little more flour. Do not over-knead!
6. Transfer dough to a lightly floured surface and shape into a round loaf. the dough will be a little sticky, and quite shaggy.
7. You want to work it just enough so that the flour is just moistened and the dough just barely comes together. Shaggy is good. If you over-knead, the bread will end up tough.
8. Transfer dough to a large, lightly greased cast-iron skillet or a baking sheet.
9. Using a serrated knife, score top of dough about an inch and a half deep in an X shape. The purpose of the scoring is to help heat get into the center of the dough while it cooks.
10. Transfer to oven and bake at 425°F until bread is golden and bottom sounds hollow when tapped, about 35-45 minutes.
11. Check for doneness also by inserting a long, thin skewer into the center. If it comes out clean, it's done.
12. Remove pan or sheet from oven, let bread sit in the pan or on the sheet for 5-10 minutes, then remove to a rack to cool briefly.

Serving Suggestion: Serve bread warm, at room temperature, or sliced and toasted. Best when eaten warm and just baked.

Variation Tip: Add almonds for variation.

Nutritional Information per Serving:

Calories 172.6|Carbohydrates 34g|Protein 5.1g|Fat 2.1g|Sodium 279.1mg|Fiber 1.4g

Herby Roast Chicken and Onion-Garlic Mashed Potatoes

Prep Time: 30 minutes | Cook Time: 20 minutes + 30 minutes cooling time | Servings: 18

Ingredients:

Herby Chicken:

1 small onion, sliced	¼ teaspoon dried thyme
1 whole chicken	¼ teaspoon dried sage
2 tablespoons butter, softened	¼ teaspoon dried basil
2 cloves garlic, minced	Salt and pepper
½ teaspoon dried parsley	½ cup water

Onion-Garlic Mashed Potatoes:

1 ¼ pound potatoes, diced	2 cloves garlic, minced
4 tablespoons butter, divided	¼ - ½ cup milk
1 small onion, minced	Salt

Preparation:

1. Preheat the oven to 400°F. Place the onions in the bottom of a baking dish. Mix together the softened butter, garlic, and herbs. Place the chicken in the baking dish on top of the onions.

2. Gently loosen the skin of the chicken. Rub the butter mixture both over and under the chicken skin.

3. Season the chicken with salt and pepper and add the water to the bottom of the baking dish. Cover and bake for 50 minutes.

4. Rotate the pan, uncover, and increase heat to 425°F. Continue baking for another 30 minutes or until a thermometer inserted into the thickest part of the thigh reads 170°F.

5. As the chicken cooks, prepare the potatoes.

6. Place 1 tablespoon of butter in a skillet over medium-low heat. Add the onions and cook, stirring frequently until they begin to caramelize, reaching a deep amber color. Toward the end of cooking, add the garlic, and cook for another 2-3 minutes. Remove from heat and set aside.

7. Cook the potatoes in a large pot of boiling salted water. Cook for 20 minutes or until tender. Drain and pour into a bowl.

8. Add the onion mixture to the potatoes. Add the remaining butter and ¼ cup milk and mash by hand. If the potatoes are too thick, add additional milk. Season with salt and serve with the chicken.

Serving Suggestion: Serve the herby chicken with onion garlic mashed potatoes.

Variation Tip: Sprinkle herbs on the mashed potatoes and additional butter if you desire.

Nutritional Information per Serving:

Calories 581 | Carbohydrates 51g | Protein 46g | Fat 21g | Sodium 30mg | Fiber 0g

Cornish Shepherd's Pie

Prep Time: 20 minutes|Cook Time: 1 hour 30 minutes|Servings: 4

Ingredients:

16 ounces ground beef or lamb

½ cup onion, chopped

½ cup tomato, chopped

½ cup green bell pepper, chopped

2 carrots, chopped

2 tablespoons garlic, minced

2 celery ribs, chopped

1 tablespoon thyme

1 tablespoon fresh parsley, chopped

¾ cup tomato paste

¼ cup flour

2 cups beef broth

½ cup sherry

1 teaspoon Worcestershire sauce

1 teaspoon paprika

1 teaspoon chicken base or stock

2 teaspoons balsamic vinegar

1 packet instant garlic mashed potatoes

2 tablespoons butter

Salt and pepper, to taste

Preparation:

1. Brown the meat with some oil in a skillet over medium heat.

2. Remove the meat from the skillet.

3. Add the onion to the skillet and fry for about 3–5 minutes.

4. Add the bell peppers, celery, carrots, and garlic. Cook for another 4 minutes.

5. Add the tomatoes and flour. Mix well.

6. Stir in the tomato paste.

7. Take a bowl, and add the beef broth, Worcestershire sauce, paprika, chicken base, balsamic vinegar, salt, and pepper. Stir to mix.

8. Add the mixture to the skillet and add the meat. Cook for about 20–30 minutes.

9. Preheat the oven to 400°F.

10. Prepare the mashed potatoes as per the packet instructions.

11. Place the meat mixture in a baking dish and spread the mashed potatoes on top.

12. Place the baking dish in the oven and bake for about 30–40 minutes.

13. Serve and enjoy!

Serving Suggestions: Serve with a side salad.

Variation Tip: You can also add cayenne pepper.

Nutritional Information per Serving:

Calories: 684|Fat: 41.38g|Sat Fat: 17.36g|Carbohydrates: 55.93g|Fiber: 7.5g|Sugar: 12.23g|Protein: 24.13g

First Feast Roasted Turkey

Prep Time: 20 minutes|Cook Time: 3 hours 30 minutes|Servings: 16

Ingredients

12 to 20 pounds turkey	quartered
1 onion, peeled and quartered	¾ ounce fresh rosemary
1 lemon, quartered	¾ ounce fresh thyme
1 apple (your favourite kind),	¾ ounce fresh sage

For the herb butter

1 cup unsalted butter,	black pepper
softened	6 to 8 cloves garlic, minced
1 teaspoon salt	fresh chopped herbs
½ teaspoon freshly ground	

Preparation

1. Adjust your oven rack so the turkey will sit in the center of the oven.

2. Preheat oven to 325°F.

3. Make the herb butter by combining room temperature butter, minced garlic, salt, pepper, fresh chopped rosemary, fresh chopped thyme, and fresh chopped sage.

4. Remove the neck and giblets from the inside of the turkey. Pat the turkey with paper towels until it is completely dry.

5. Season the cavity of the turkey with salt and pepper. Stuff it with the quartered lemon, onion and apple and leftover herbs.

6. Use your fingers to loosen and lift the skin above the breasts on the top of the turkey and gently put in a few tablespoon of the herb butter underneath.

7. Tuck the wings of the turkey underneath the turkey and set the turkey on a roasting rack inside a roasting pan.

8. Microwave the remaining herb butter mixture for 30 seconds. Use a basting brush to brush the remaining herb butter all over the outside of the turkey, legs and wings.

9. Roast at 325°F for about 13 to 15 minutes per pound, or until internal temperature (inserted on middle of thigh and breast reaches about 165°F.)

10. Check the turkey about halfway through the baking process, and once the skin gets golden brown, cover the top of the turkey with tinfoil, to protect the breast meat from overcooking.

11. Allow turkey to rest for 20 to 30 minutes before carving.

Serving Suggestion: Serve hot with chilled butter beer.
Variation Tip: Substitute fresh herbs to dry if not available.
Nutritional Information Per Serving:
Calories 576|Carbohydrates 3g|Protein 70g|Fat 30g|Sodium 518mg|Fiber 5g

Conclusion

Thank you for purchasing this cookbook! If you love the wizard series, this cookbook is perfect for you. In this cookbook, you'll find delicious wizard-inspired recipes. Each recipe has step-by-step cooking instructions, prep/cook time, number of servings, and a beautiful recipe final dish image. In this cookbook, you will find Top Magical Food at the Wizard World, Magical Recipe Terms, Questions for your Kids if They Love Wizard Series, Wizard Essentials, History of Magic, and What to Serve at Your Hogwarts Dinner Feast in this cookbook. You can make a wizard theme for a birthday party. You can prepare wizard recipes for different occasions. Enjoy these recipes on different occasions. Welcome to the magical food world!

Appendix 1 Measurement Conversion Chart

WEIGHT EQUIVALENTS

US STANDARD	METRIC (APPROXINATE)
1 ounce	28 g
2 ounces	57 g
5 ounces	142 g
10 ounces	284 g
15 ounces	425g
16 ounces (1 pound)	455 g
1.5 pounds	680 g
2 pounds	907 g

VOLUME EQUIVALENTS (LIQUID)

US STANDARD	US STANDARD (OUNCES)	METRIC (APPROXIMATE)
2 tablespoons	1 fl.oz	30 mL
¼ cup	2 fl.oz	60 mL
½ cup	4 fl.oz	120 mL
1 cup	8 fl.oz	240 mL
1½ cup	12 fl.oz	355 mL
2 cups or 1 pint	16 fl.oz	475 mL
4 cups or 1 quart	32 fl.oz	1 L
1 gallon	128 fl.oz	4 L

VOLUME EQUIVALENTS (DRY)

US STANDARD	METRIC (APPROXIMATE)
⅛ teaspoon	0.5 mL
¼ teaspoon	1 mL
½ teaspoon	2 mL
¾ teaspoon	4 mL
1 teaspoon	5 mL
1 tablespoon	15 mL
¼ cup	59 mL
½ cup	118 mL
¾ cup	177 mL
1 cup	235 mL
2 cups	475 mL
3 cups	700 mL
4 cups	1 L

TEMPERATURES EQUIVALENTS

FAHRENHEIT (F)	CELSIUS (C) (APPROXIMATE)
225 ℉	107℃
250 ℉	120℃
275 ℉	135℃
300 ℉	150℃
325 ℉	160℃
350 ℉	180℃
375 ℉	190℃
400 ℉	205℃
425 ℉	220℃
450 ℉	235℃
475 ℉	245℃
500 ℉	260℃

Appendix 2 Recipes Index